Pebbles
from the *Brink*

by M.C. Pritchard

ISBN 0-921702-83-3
Special Crossroads Edition, 1998
Published by Crossroads Christian Communications Inc.
P.O. Box 5100, Burlington, Ontario, Canada L7R 4M2
Used by permission.

First published in 1913
Holiness Movement Print
Ottawa, Ontario

ST. PAUL - A.D. 66

"I have fought a good fight, I have finished my course, I have kept the faith: Henceforth there is laid up for me a crown of righteousness, which the Lord, the righteous Judge, shall give me at that day: and not to me only, but unto all them also that love His appearing."   2 Timothy 4:7,8

FOREWORD

How well I remember being filled with pride when my grade six class at Mutchmore Public School in Ottawa filed past a mounted albino deer placed in the Canada Museum of Natural History. I pointed out that the name on the plaque below the deer was M.C. Pritchard, my Uncle Manly. He was also my minister at that time in the Fifth Avenue Holiness Movement Church.

Uncle Manly was my favourite. He always had great stories to illustrate his sermons. A lot of those stories came from the Laurentian Mountains in an area of Quebec north of Ottawa where he was born in 1876. My mother came along 22 years later in 1898. In the wintertime they would step out the door every morning, climb onto a sleigh and slide down the mountain for a mile, ending up right at the one-room schoolhouse. Of course, the journey home wasn't quite so much fun!

Many of my favourite memories are from the mountainside farmhouse. I think I might remember being the youngest child at Great-Grandmother Hall's 100th birthday party in 1938. She was almost 30 when Canada became a country in 1867. These are some of my roots on my mother's side of the family.

Uncle Manly, Rev. M.C. Pritchard, began preaching for the Methodists before the turn of the century and around that time joined the "Holiness Movement," a revival branch of Methodism, that by 1910 claimed 10,000 adherents in Canada.

He served numerous "circuits." A circuit was a Methodist word for several congregations that shared one minister. During his extensive travels throughout Quebec and Ontario by horse and buggy, he sat with many people who were dying. Often they were in remote areas without a medical doctor in attendance. Of course, there was no medication to dull the mind and many had profound words to say — both good and bad — just before passing. These insights into life here and in the hereafter interested him sufficiently that he began to compile from his own experience and from the experience of others, the sayings of the dying. He first published "Pebbles From The Brink" in 1913. He shares his reason for this title in his introduction. For years now, I have wanted to republish my uncle's book, and now here it is.

I've received from Dr. Maurice Rawlings, M.D. some modern deathbed sayings which I've included. For years this eminent heart specialist, and one-time physician to Generals Eisenhower and Marshall, has spent night after night in the emergency wards of the great university hospitals, teaching students and interns resuscitation techniques. He pioneered some of these techniques himself, such as threading electrodes inside the heart to produce an electric shock to jump-start the heart. The "pebbles from the brink" that Dr. Rawlings has found are also, in the words of M.C. Pritchard, both "diamonds and cinders."

I want to write a conclusion at the back of this book. It is my hope that "Pebbles From The Brink" will interest you, shock you, and change you as it has me.

David Mainse
March, 1998

Special Note:

During the week of March, 1998, it was our honour to have with us on "100 Huntley Street" the man who is probably the world's most-beloved Gospel singer, George Beverly Shea. He shared with us about his father's last words:

> *"My sister Pauline came into his room just to minister to him. 'Pauline, do you hear the music?' he asked. 'What music, Dad?' she responded. He replied, 'Oh, you wouldn't know,' and went to be with the Lord."*

George also shared about his grandfather:

> *"The doctor came into the room and said, 'George, quit singing. That's hard on you.' He was singing these words on his deathbed: 'When I've gone the last mile of the way, I will rest at the close of the day....' Then his voice faded, and he was gone."*

INTRODUCTION

In conveying truth, testimony is one of the chiefest factors. How anxious the tradesman is to obtain testimony to his efficiency; the manufacturer to the value of his goods; the physician to his skill. Why this testimony seeking? Because testimony is convincing. Testimony is born of experience, and is the expression of experimental knowledge.

The disciples wisely declared, "We cannot but speak the things which we have seen and heard." They heard the Word of God, saw the miracles of Jesus, and left a soul-stirring testimony on record. Testimony is borne not only by the animate, but also by the inanimate: the rocks, valleys, sun, moon, stars.... Everything in nature bears infallible proof to the great truths which surround us.

The object of this book is simply to record the varied emotions of souls nearing the river crossing. I have entitled these testimonies, "pebbles," as they are as varied as those to be found on the ocean shore. Some are rare and beautiful, reflecting the colours of the rainbow or the sparkle of the dewdrop; others are dark and unattractive. Often a pebble of small dimensions is of priceless value; so, many testimonies herein recorded, contain the beautiful, the joyous, the rich and the rare.

"From The Brink" - This is a river we must all cross. The testimony of travellers who were about to pass over, prove to us that death may be the opening of a gate into the "City of God" or a door that leads to the "corridors of hell."

It is my earnest hope that "Pebbles From The Brink" may be a means in the hands of God of awakening souls and helping them to walk soberly in this life; thus enabling them to experience, not fear, but rapturous joy at the border of the river!

M. C. Pritchard
Smith's Falls, Ontario
April 9, 1913

The day of one's birth is laden with interest. With each birth a new life has been introduced to an existence on this mundane sphere; a body enveloping a priceless gem, an immortal spirit. This compound being has been launched upon the ocean of life. A voyage, more or less exciting; yet fraught with many problems, cares, anxieties, toils, sufferings and the dangers that lie before. Whether it will reach the allotted "three score and ten," or fade in the bloom of youth, none but God and heaven knows.

At any rate, there is an ending of the voyage. As our birth introduced us to this earthly life, so death will introduce us to an eternal existence — either with God and holy angels in heaven or with foul demons and all the unholy in the regions of eternal despair. Which, oh, which, will it be?

This worthy volume contains a collation of the last sayings of a great number of those whose earthly pilgrimage is drawing to a close. The end, to some, is in full view. Memories of a lifetime seem to crowd themselves into one short moment.

To many, the glorious prospects of eternal bliss are bursting in upon their vision. They have sighted their beautiful home. Angels are waiting, loved ones are beckoning. The gates are ajar. You, who would make heaven your home, read their last words and take on fresh inspiration and courage.

But sad, sad it is for others to whom eternal night and endless despair are just as real. Even those who scoffed the idea of

God and heaven and hell now believe in all, and moan, "Too late! Too late!"

You, who are careless and without hope, read their last doleful words, take warning and prepare for the solemn moment.

Such a volume as is placed before us must have occasioned a vast amount of research. At first we thought the word "pebbles" should have been "pearls," but for obvious reasons it was not.

It is our desire that this book speed forth as a white-winged harbinger of divine peace into thousands of homes. May each reader — when life's short day is ended — with exultant vision, behold the gates of the celestial city ajar and receive an abundant entrance!

G.A. Christie
Holiness Movement Print, 1913

JESUS OUR SAVIOUR - A.D. 33

Having arrived at the place of execution, the condemned was stripped and fastened to the cross, which was usually of the form familiar to us under the name of the Roman cross. The body was either bound or nailed to the cross, or in both ways. Our Lord was nailed by the hands and feet as the prophet had foretold; a method more exquisitely painful at first, though tending to shorten the torture.

When the cross was already standing, the sufferer was raised up and affixed to it; but otherwise, as in our Saviour's case, he was fastened to it as it lay upon the ground, and the shock when it dropped into the hole or socket must have been terrible. To deaden the sense of these tortures, a solution with anaesthetic properties was usually administered, but our Lord refused to partake of it. He still observed the meek silence that Isaiah had foretold till all the horrid details were accomplished.

Jesus hung upon the cross between the two malefactors— one on His right, and one on His left. It was there that He uttered a prayer for His murderers, the first of the seven sayings which have been revered as His dying words: "Father, forgive them for they know not what they do."

The second time His lips were opened with words of assurance to the penitent thief: "Verily, I say unto thee, today thou shalt be with Me in paradise." Having thus forgiven His persecutors, and blessed the penitent sinner, our Lord spoke for the third time in tender care of those dear to Him on earth.

It was now noon, but such a noon as had never been seen in Judea. Darkness rested on all the land. But far deeper than that darkness was the gloom that weighed upon the Saviour's soul, as He bore the whole burden of the divine wrath for the sins of all mankind. To that awful mystery, our only guide is in the words, with which at the ninth hour He broke the solemn silence: "My God, My God, why hast thou forsaken Me?" A little later the sufferer's mortal frame endured its last agony of intense thirst, and to fulfill one more prophecy, He exclaimed, "I thirst."

And now all that man could inflict had been endured; all that the Son of God could do and bear for mankind had been done and suffered. The end of His agony, and the completion of His redeeming work are both announced by the loud cry, "It is finished!" The soul which had animated His mortal body is yielded back to God with those words of perfect resignation: "Father, into Thy hands I commend My spirit"; and bowing His head upon His breast, He expired.

STEPHEN - A.D. 33
While being stoned for his testimony of the Gospel, Stephen looked up to heaven and said: "Behold I see the heavens opened, and the Son of man standing on the right hand of God." At this the mob rushed upon him, and he kneeled down, and cried with a loud voice, "Lord, lay not this sin to their charge." And when he had said this, he fell asleep.

WILLIAM ALLEN - A.D. 1843
"How often I think of those precious words of the Saviour, 'That they may be with me where I am.'"

LADY MARY FITZGERALD - A.D. 1815

When she was nearly 90 years old, her clothes caught fire, and her servants, hastening to her, found her wrapped in flames. She lingered till the next day with a faith which triumphed over her agonies. "I might as well go home this way as any other," she said to her family. Her last words were, "Come, Lord Jesus, my blessed Redeemer; come, and receive my spirit."

ADDISON - A.D. 1719

When given up by his physicians, Addison sent for his stepson, the young Earl of Warwick. Grasping his hand very impressively he said to him, "See how a Christian can die!"

LEONARD KEYSER - A.D. 1527

He was burned at Scherding as a martyr. Looking at the crowd, he exclaimed, "Behold the harvest! Oh Master, send forth Thy labourers!"

AULD PEGGIE

Auld Peggie, after having had the Gospel of the grace of God faithfully presented to her by a Christian minister, put down her pipe and anxiously weighed the matter over. By and by she resumed her pipe; her face was callous and unmoved. She then slowly said, "Na, na; I've lived without Him 70 years; and I can live without Him the rest o' my days!"

Shortly after she was found dead in bed, the pipe broken on the floor, and her withered arms thrown above her head, as if there had been some fearful conflict with an unseen foe.

COLONEL CHARTERIS
"I would gladly give £30,000 to have it proved to my satisfaction that there is no such a place as hell."

ABRAHAM ALBRECHT - A.D. 1815
"I go to Jesus; I am a member of His body."

MARY FLETCHER - A.D. 1815
On the 9th of December she entered into her eternal rest. Among her last utterances were, "I am drawing near to glory.... There is my home and portion fair.... Jesus come, my hope of glory.... He lifts His hands, and shows that I am graven there." Then she said to a Christian friend, "The Lord bless both thee and me," and died.

ALTAMONT
"My principles have poisoned my friends, my extravagance has beggared my boy, my unkindness has murdered my wife, and is there another hell? Oh, Thou blasphemed, yet most indulgent Lord God, hell itself is a refuge if it hides me from Thy frown!"

THOS. RUTHERFORD - A.D. 1806
"He has indeed been a precious Christ to me, and now I feel Him to be my rock, my strength, my rest, my hope, my joy, my all in all!"

REV. ALEXANDER MATHER - A.D. 1800
His last days were attended with extreme suffering, but with equal triumph. Shortly before he expired, he cried out in extreme anguish, "I long to be gone! I long to be gone! I am

happy in Jesus, but my sufferings are very great!"

Nearly the last words he uttered were: "I now know that I have not sought Thee in vain. I have not — I have not — I have not! Oh, Thou, that causest light to shine out of darkness, shine upon my soul with the light of the knowledge of the Son of God. The Name above every other name, forever dear, it dispels all my fears. Oh, proclaim Jesus! Tell me, shall I be with Him this night?"

On being answered, "Yes, there is little doubt of it," he cried out, "He that I have served for nearly 50 years will not forsake me now. Glory be to God and the Lamb forever and ever! Amen! Amen! Amen!" His voice slowly failed. He seemed to sink into a tranquil slumber, and almost imperceptibly passed away.

CHARLES BALA - A.D. 1814
"There is a refuge."

JOHN PAYSON - A.D. 1806
His dying chamber was an extraordinary, sublime scene. He cried out, "It is enough. Christ died for me. I am mounting up to the throne of God!" Then breaking forth in rapturous strains of praise, and clasping his hands, he said, "I know I am dying, but my deathbed is a bed of roses. I have no thorns planted on my dying pillow. Heaven already is begun. Everlasting life is won... is won... is won. I die a safe, easy, happy death. Thou, my God, art present, I know. I feel Thou art. Precious Jesus! Glory! Glory be to God!" Soon after he died exclaiming, "My God! My God! My God!"

CHARLES CHURCHILL - A.D. 1764
Davies relates that his last words were, "What a fool I have been!"

CHRYSOSTOM - A.D. 407
"Glory be to God for all things that happen! Amen."

JOHN VALTON - A.D. 1794
Agonizing sufferings could not baffle his spiritual victory. Whoever entered his chamber, found that he was still a preacher. Another aged preacher, Richard Rodda, called to see him on his deathbed. The dying evangelist stretched out his hand to receive him, exclaiming, "Welcome, welcome, blessed servant of the Lord! I am happy; I am happy!"

Then he said to a later visitor, "Oh, my brother, for the last four days my soul has been in a state of inward glory." On being asked if he suffered much pain, his answer was, "Pain is not affliction, but a blessing."

"Prayer!" he exclaimed. "I have done with prayer now. I can love. I can praise. But I cannot pray." Uttering the words so often on the lips of dying saints, he said, "Now, Lord, lettest Thou Thy servant depart in peace; for my eyes have seen Thy salvation." He fell asleep in Jesus.

LADY MAXWELL
"My peace is inexpressibly sweet."

MARGARET GAMBLE - A.D. 1905
The day previous to her death, she called her loved ones

around her bed and exhorted all to be at their best for God. She continued, telling them to stand true to the end and to meet her in heaven. Then she kissed one after another a last farewell, bidding them not to weep, but to rejoice with her.

For some time she remained silent, as if her mind were too much absolved in heavenly things to notice earthly scenes. Later on she said, "Where is my sweet love?" meaning her little granddaughter. "I want her to sing two favourite hymns for me."

With a sweet smile she watched the child while singing in tremulous strains, the beautiful words, "Oh such wonderful love!" and "There's not a friend like the lowly Jesus." Then she said, "Oh that lifts me up to heaven!" At times a smile would play over her features, as though an unseen hand had lifted the thin veil between her and glory. Among her last utterances were, "Jesus is with me all the time. The sting of death is taken away. All is light and liberty."

After this her words were inaudible. A solemn stillness settled down upon her and, in a few moments more, the pearly gates opened to receive her happy spirit.

SIR ISAAC NEWTON - A.D. 1727
Shortly before his death he said, "I do not know what I may appear to the world; but to myself, I seem to have been only like a boy playing on the seashore: diverting himself by now and then, finding a smooth pebble or a prettier shell than ordinary, while the great ocean of truth lies all undiscovered beyond me."

JESSIE
"Yes, I shall soon be at home." Then she added quickly, "Not to the hills of Fife; but to see His face."

DR. NETTLETON - A.D. 1844
"While ye have the light, walk in the light."

HAYDEN - A.D. 1809
"God preserve the Emperor!"

MRS. ALBERT RENNIE - A.D. 1905
The last words we heard her say were, "Bless the Lord, oh my soul, and all that is within me, bless His holy name." She then clapped her hands twice, and repeated Jesus' name, and in a little while she was gone.

ROBERT FLOCKHART
"How I'll make the arches of heaven ring with loud hallelujahs to God and the Lamb."

THOMAS ROGERSON - A.D. 1836
After nearly half a century in the ministry, he died saying, "All is right; all is well!"

R. HAZELL
"What have we to fear? All fullness dwells in Christ."

PHILIP J. JENKS
A friend said to him, just before he expired, "How hard it is to die!" "Oh, no, no, no!" he replied. "Easy dying! Blessed dying! Glorious dying! I have experienced more happiness two

hours today while dying, than in my whole life. I have long desired that I might glorify God in my death. But, oh, I never thought that such a poor worm as I, could come to such a glorious death!"

PHILIP DE MORNACY
"Alas! What was there of mine in that work? Say not that it was I, but God by me. I laboured yet not I, but the grace of God which was in me. Away with all merit, either in me or any other man whatsoever. I call for nothing but mercy; free mercy!"

JEROME - A.D. 146
"This soul in flames, I offer, Christ, to Thee!"

SHENADOAH
Shenadoah was an Oneida chief who died when over 100 years old. For 50 years he had lived a Christian life. "I am an aged hemlock. The winds of 100 years have whistled through my branches. I am dead at the top (he was blind). Why I yet live the great good Spirit knows. Pray to my Jesus that I may wait with patience my appointed time. And when I die lay me by the side of my minister and father, that I may go up with him at the great resurrection."

JAMES NEEDHAM
"Glory, honour, might, majesty, and dominion be ascribed to God and the Lamb, forever and ever."

REV. ROBERT NEWTON, D.D.
He died on April 30, 1854 at the age of 73. His difficulty of

breathing increased, and it was evident that the last conflict was begun. He made an attempt to speak, and we could only catch a few disjointed sentences, such as, "I am the Resurrection... God... Jesus Christ... the ransom of sinners... life from the dead... praise the Lord, praise Him... praise Him, all the earth."

In about an hour he sank exhausted. His lips moved, as if in prayer. He folded his hands on his breast, and was heard pouring out his soul for his family. By putting the ear close to his mouth we heard distinctly his dying testimony:

"I am going to leave you, but God will be with you. Jesus is the resurrection and the life; and the life of Jesus is life from the dead. The effectual, fervent prayer of a righteous man availeth much. By their prayers they shall prevail; by their prayers and tears. Hear Thou, their prayers and tears. Blessed is the righteous in his life, and in his death. He shall see Jesus in the day when all tears are wiped away, and sorrow and crying are no more. The righteous shall never die. Fear sin, not death. Farewell! I am going to join the myriads of angels and archangels before the throne of God. Farewell sin and farewell death. Praise the Lord! Praise Him forever!"

After another interval, he again made an effort to speak; and we heard him say, "Praise God! Praise!" At one o'clock on Saturday afternoon, the voice that had so often led the prayers and praises of religious assemblies was hushed forever.

DOUGLAS JERROLD - A.D. 1857
"I feel as one who is waiting, and waited for."

JOHN WILSON PIPE - A.D. 1836
"I am upon the rock, Christ; only Christ."

HUGO GROTIUS - A.D. 1645
"Be serious."

GIBBON - A. D. 1794
"All is dark and doubtful."

EUNICE COBB - A.D. 1879
A Christian friend who visited her three hours before her death says, "Her dress had always been blue calico, and an old-fashioned Methodist bonnet. I said to her, 'Mother Cobb, you have been very particular about your dress, don't you think more so than necessary?' She replied, 'No, brother, it pays, it pays.' Finally, her last words were, 'Victory! Victory! Eternal victory!'"

MR. D.
"Think of me tomorrow, as the happiest being you ever heard of."

RICHARD MOSS
"I'm going now; good-bye. The Lord bless you. I am so happy."

QUEEN ELIZABETH - A.D. 1602
"All my possessions for a moment of time!"

ROBERT BURNS - A.D. 1835

The expiring poet whispered to a friend by his bedside, "I may have but a moment to speak to you, my dear. Be a good man. Be virtuous, be religious; nothing else will give you any comfort, when you come to be here."

ISABELLA CAMPBELL

"I want my dear brother-in-Christ to be present and engage in prayer when my spirit flies to glory. Saviour, Saviour!"

JOSEPH TAYLOR - A.D. 1830

One of Wesley's heroes, and 53 years a preacher, he said, "I can talk of nothing but the love of Christ."

JOSEPH ROBINSON - A.D. 1832

"I'm going to Jesus."

BENJAMIN PIERCE - A.D. 1794

On his way to Barbados after preaching in England, Ireland, and the West Indies, he died of a putrid fever. Calling the captain of the vessel to his side, he exclaimed, "Tell my friends in Barbados that I died happy in God," and expired.

DUKE OF HAMILTON - A.D. 1649

"Douglas, in a little time you shall be a duke, and I shall be a king."

ZACHARIAH YEDVDALL - A.D. 1830

He expired shouting, "God is love! Jesus is precious! I am going to God!"

DR. HENRY HAMMOND - A.D. 1660
"Lord, make haste!"

JOSEPH CONLEY - A.D. 1792
"It is better for me to be dissolved, that I may be with Jesus," he said. Then he died without a struggle or groan.

JOHN TRETHEWY
"All is fixed; everything is settled, and God is with me. There is no doubt upon my mind; no, not the least."

WILLIAM HARRISON - A.D. 1835
After nearly 45 years in the itinerancy, he died saying, "I stand upon the rock!"

ROBERT LOWE
"I am going. My eyesight is almost gone. Brighter and brighter."

HENRY II - A.D. 1024
"Henceforth, let all things go as they may; I care nothing more about myself or the world." He raised himself convulsively half up in bed and with a wild look, bewailed his son, who had deserted him. Then turning his face to the wall, he fell back upon the bed.

OLIVER GOLDSMITH - A.D. 1774
When asked, "Is your mind at ease?" the dying man replied, "No, it is not!"

JOHN CALVIN - A.D. 1564

"Thou, Lord, bruisest me; but I am abundantly satisfied, since it is from Thy hand!"

THOMAS OSBORN - A.D. 1836

He departed declaring, "I shall go down to the grave with a smile, and ascend with a shout."

DAVID BRAINERD - A.D. 1747

"My delight is to please God and be wholly devoted to His glory. That is the heaven I long for, that is my religion and my happiness, and always was — ever since I suppose I ever had any true religion.... The Watcher is with me. Why is the chariot so long in coming? Look forth. Why tarry the wheels of His chariot?"

HENRY V - A.D. 1422

"If I had finished the war in France and established peace, I would have gone to Palestine to redeem the holy city from Saracens."

SIR JAMES MACKINTOSH - A.D. 1832

"I believe in Jesus."

EARL OF BUCHAN - A.D. 1829

"Happy! Happy!"

EDWARD III - A.D. 1377

What with the weakness of the king's body, the contrition of his heart, and the sobbing for his sins, his voice and speech failed him. Scarcely pronouncing the word "Jesus," he, with this last word, made an end of his speech, and expired.

MATTHEW HENRY - A.D. 1714
"A life spent in the service of God and communion with Him is the most comfortable life that anyone can live in this present world."

MRS. HEARNE
"Hallelujah! Hallelujah! Hallelujah to God and the Lamb, forever and ever and ever!"

DR. KITTS - A.D. 1854
"Pray to God to take me soon."

DUNCAN WRIGHT - A.D. 1791
On his deathbed, he remarked that at a given time he had entered into "a superior light and greater liberty than he had ever enjoyed before." From that hour he walked constantly in the light of God's countenance, and could not be satisfied any day without a direct and clear witness of his acceptance with God.

"I am a witness," he added, "that the blood of Christ does cleanse from all sin. Oh the goodness of God to a poor sinner! The Lord has finished His work, has cleansed me and filled me with His fullness. Oh what a weight of glory will that be, since Thy weight of grace, oh Lord, is now so great!"

He suffered much, but was undismayed at death. "Jesus is come!" he at last exclaimed, and died while a group of his brethren were kneeling at his bedside. He was buried in

Wesley's own tomb, in the City Road graveyard.

HAPPY JOHN, A POLICEMAN
He was a great sufferer, yet in departing said, "I was never so happy before! Finished.... Completed.... Blood.... Face to face!"

SIR PHILIP SYDNEY - A.D. 1586
Seeing a soldier lying near, mangled like himself, and dying, this amiable and accomplished gentleman refused water offered to him, saying, "Give it to that poor man; his sufferings are greater than mine." His last utterance was, "In me behold the end of this world, with all its vanities."

JOHN BROWN - A.D. 1786
"Oh, commend Jesus! There is none like Christ; none like Christ!"

GENERAL HAVELOCK - A.D. 1857
"Come, my son, and see how a Christian can die."

JOHN BROWN OF HADDINGTON - A.D. 1787
"My Christ; my Christ!"

SAMMY HICK - A.D. 1829
On his deathbed a friend asked him, "What must we say to your friends who enquire after you?" He answered, "Tell them that I have all packed up; that I am still in the old ship, with my anchor cast within the veil, and that my sails are up, filled with a heavenly breeze. In a short time I shall be launched into the heavenly ocean." On the night of November 9th, 1829, he said, "I am going!" and died.

GOLDING

His brother said to him, "You seem to enjoy a foretaste of heaven." He replied, "Oh, this is not a foretaste; this is heaven! I not only feel the climate, but I breathe the fine ambrosial air of heaven, and soon shall enjoy the company." His last words were, "Glory! Glory! Glory!"

WILLIAM HICK - A.D. 1834

"I do not die; I depart."

JOHN SMITH - A.D. 1832

"All is clear," he said to one of his colleagues. "I have had some success in my labours, but my happiness does not result from that, but from this: I have now hold of God. I am a very great sinner, yet saved by the wonderful love of God in Christ Jesus. I throw my person and my labours at His feet."

JOHN RICHARDSON - A.D. 1791

Like his Master, he was a man of sorrows and acquainted with grief. After suffering for 26 years of severe asthma (which would not keep him from the pulpit), he died uttering as his last words: "God is always with me!"

A LITTLE GIRL

"Jesus Christ said to me, 'Come,' and so I came to Him. And now I say to Jesus, 'Come,' and He will come very soon and will send His angels, and will carry me away."

JOHN WESLEY - A.D. 1791

As the friends gathered around his dying bed, he attempted to speak; but observing that he could not be understood, he paused and, collecting his strength, exclaimed, "The best of all is, God is with us." A witness of the scene then observed his final words and actions:

"Lifting up his dying arms in a token of victory, and raising his feeble voice with a holy triumph, not to be expressed, he cried out, 'The best of all is, God is with us.' On being informed that the widow of Charles Wesley had come, he said, in allusion to his deceased brother, 'He giveth His servants rest.' He then thanked her, as she pressed his hand, and affectionately endeavoured to kiss her.

"As they wet his lips, he said, 'We thank Thee, O Lord, for these and all Thy mercies. Bless the Church and king, and grant us truth and peace, through Jesus Christ our Lord, forever and ever!' Some of his broken but rapturous utterances in these last hours were: 'He causeth His servants to lie down in peace....The clouds drop fatness....The Lord is with us....The God of Jacob is our refuge.'

"Again he summoned the company to prayer at his bedside. The chamber had become not merely a sanctuary, but it seemed the gate of heaven. He joined in the service with increased fervour. During the night he attempted frequently to repeat the hymn of Watts, which he had sung the preceding day but could only now utter, 'I'll praise.... I'll praise....'"

The next morning the sublime scene closed. Joseph Bradford, long his ministerial travelling companion, the sharer of his trials and successes, prayed with him.

"Farewell!" was the last word and benediction of the dying apostle.

CATO - B.C. 148
"Have my friends yet embarked? Does anything yet remain that could be done to save them?" He had exhorted his friends to save themselves. And after enquiring as above, he dismissed his servant, stabbed himself, and expired.

QUEEN CAROLINE - A.D. 1821
"Open the window! Pray." Princess Emily began to read a prayer; but before she had read ten words, the Queen had passed away.

BISHOP GARDINER - A.D. 1555
Gardiner delayed dinner on the day of the martyrdom of Ridley and Latimer until he received the account of their burning. At this meal, the first severe symptoms of fatal disease manifested themselves, a disorder which rapidly increased. It was of so disgusting a character, that it was scarcely possible to get anyone to come near him. His last words were, "I have sinned, like Peter, but have not wept like him."

LORD HARANT
Approaching the block, he kneeled down, and exclaimed: "Into Thy hands, oh Lord, I commend my spirit! In Thee have I always trusted. Receive me, therefore, my blessed Redeemer!"

JOHN STAMP - A.D. 1831
"All is well!"

NAPOLEON BONAPARTE - A.D. 1821
To Count de Montholon, he said, "I die before my time, and my body will be given back to the earth to become food for worms. Such is the fate of him who has been called the great Napoleon! What an abyss between my deep misery and the eternal Kingdom of Christ which is proclaimed, loved, and adored, and is extended over the whole earth."

During a terrible storm, similar to that exceptional convulsion of the elements during which he was born, the great emperor expired, uttering the words, "Mon Dieu, la nation Française, tête d'armée." (Translation: "My God, raise up a head for the army of the French nation.")

DIRICK CARVER - A.D. 1555
"Dear brethren, as many of you as do believe upon the Father, the Son, and the Holy Ghost unto everlasting life, see you do the works appertaining to the same."

JOSEPH CHAPMAN - A.D. 1833
"Glory, glory! Victory, victory!"

RAYMOND LULLY - A.D. 1315
"I was once rich, lascivious, and worldly; but willingly did I forsake everything to advance the glory of God, the good of mankind, and the holy faith. I learned Arabic, and often have departed to preach to the Saracens. For my religion I have been whipped and imprisoned. Now I am old and poor, yet

steadfast in the same purpose and, through God's grace, steadfast will I remain unto death." He was stoned by the mob of Bugia, in Africa.

MRS. BONVILL

"And now the shades of evening are closing around us...." The voice of the speaker, engaged in prayer, suddenly ceased, and prayer was lost in praise.

LORD BYRON - A.D. 1824

"Shall I sue for mercy? Come, come... no weakness... let's be a man to the last."

ANN CUTLER

She seldom addressed the people in public; yet her power was in prayer, which melted the most hardened assemblies. She was "instant in prayer." It was her habit, like the psalmist, to rise at midnight and call upon God. The time for her regular hour of waking, four o'clock, till five, she spent in "pleading for herself, the society, the preachers, and the whole Church." She died as she had lived.

On the morning of her departure, she began, before the dawn, to ascribe glory to the ever blessed Trinity, and continued saying, "Glory be to the Father, glory be to the Son, and glory be to the Holy Ghost," for a considerable time. At last, looking at her attendants, she exclaimed, "I am going to die. Glory be to God and the Lamb forever!" These were her last words.

SELDEN - A.D. 1654
At the close of his life, he declared that he had possessed himself of a treasure of books and manuscripts, yet he could rest his soul upon none other than the Scriptures.

DR. LINACRE - A.D. 1524
A little before his death, worn out with fatigue and weakness, he began to read the New Testament. On perusing the fifth, sixth and seventh chapters of St. Matthew's Gospel, he threw the book from him with much violence, exclaiming: "Either this is not the Gospel, or we are not Christians!"

GRACE AGUILAR - A.D.1847
Having learned to use her fingers in the manner of the deaf and dumb, the last time they moved it was to spell upon them, "Though He slay me, yet will I trust in Him."

REV. PEARD DICKENSON
An ordained clergyman, Rev. Dickenson laboured faithfully and died triumphantly. His last words were: "Hark! Do you not hear? They are come for me. I am ready — quite ready! Stop! Say nothing, but glory! glory!"

WILLIAM SIMPSON
He was known as "a man of great simplicity and strict uprightness," who, when dying and unable to speak, was asked to lift his hand if Jesus was precious to him. He then lifted both hands in a triumphant manner and with holy joy.

GEORGE SHADFORD - A.D. 1816

As one of the heroes of American and English Methodism, he died shouting, "Victory! Victory through the blood of the Lamb!" in the 78th year of his age and the 48th year of his ministry.

MELANCTHON

"God has brought into my mind again that sweet speech of Paul, 'If God be for us, who can be against us?'" he states. Then to his son-in-law, who was inquiring if he would need anything, he replied, "Nothing, but heaven; therefore trouble me no more with speaking to me."

ELIZABETH BARRETT BROWNING - A.D. 1861

"It is beautiful!"

S. ARMISTEAD

"I am a bruised reed, leaning upon Christ.... Light! Light! Precious Jesus!"

MICHAEL ANGELO - A.D. 1564

"I commit my soul to God, my body to the earth, my possessions to my nearest relatives. I die in the faith of Jesus Christ, and in the firm hope of a better life."

THOS. KYTE

Described as rather reserved and of deep piety, after 17 years of labour in God's vineyard, he died shouting, "Praise Him! Praise Him! Praise Him!"

JOHN CLARE (THE POET) - A.D. 1850
"I want to go home."

DR. JUDSON - A.D. 1850
"I go with the gladness of a boy, bounding away from school. I feel so strong in Christ."

EBENEZER LAWRENCE
This boy was known as a Sunday school scholar. His last words were, "I am coming. Jesus is waiting for me, and I am waiting for Him! There is the white robe! There is the crown! I am going to put it on. Farewell, Mother!"

ISAAC MYERS
"Victory! Victory! Shout victory! Nearly gone... nearly gone... almost home... I am ready! He is come. He is come!"

FRANCIS BROWNE KNIGHT
"Sweet affliction! Sweet affliction! My pain of body is indeed so great no tongue can describe it, but my joy in Christ is a thousand times greater. It is inexpressible. I long to be at home."

DR. JOHN LELAND - A.D. 1766
"I give my dying testimony to the truth of Christianity. The Gospel of Christ has raised me above the fear of death, for 'I know that my Redeemer liveth.'"

HON. FRANCIS NEWPORT
"Oh, the insufferable pangs of hell and damnation!"

R. LEISTER
"The victory is gained, the prize is won!"

EARL OF DERWENTWATER - A.D. 1716
"I forgive my enemies and hope that God will forgive me."
Then turning his head up to the executioner, he said, "After
the third time I cry, 'Sweet Jesus!' strike then, and do what is
most convenient to you." A solemn scene then ensued. The
voice of the Earl was heard to exclaim, "Sweet Jesus, receive
my spirit! Sweet Jesus, be merciful unto me! Sweet Jesus...."
The sentence was broken, and the voice forever hushed in
death.

WILLIAM HUNTER - A.D. 1825
This man who preached more than forty years, died
exclaiming, "I long to be gone; I long to be gone, that I may
enter into my Father's house."

PETER MILL - A.D. 1805
"Had I a thousand tongues, they should all be employed in
praising God; and had I a thousand lives, they should all be
devoted to Him."

CAPTAIN LEE - A.D. 1784
Prior to being executed for forgery, he said, "I leave to the
world, this mournful memento: However much a man may be
favoured by personal qualifications or distinguished mental
endowments, genius will be useless, and abilities avail little,
unless accompanied by a sense of religion, and attended by
the practice of virtue."

REV. S. LEIGH
"But for confidence in Christ, I should even now be upset; but though He slay me, yet will I trust in Him."

LORD NELSON - A.D. 1805
"Kiss me, Hardy. Thank God, I have done my duty!"

EDWARD IRVING - A.D. 1834
"In life and in death I am the Lord's."

HUGO (A CHRISTIAN)
"The blessed Jesus never leaves me. Glory to His name!" And then from the pale lips rang out shout after shout of holy triumph. The room was filled with friends who knew and loved Hugo. "Come, come," he cried. "Oh, that all the world would come to Jesus! Oh, if I could tell them what He has done for me." And shout after shout came from the dying lips till they were stilled in death, while the light of heaven rested on the white face. Thus passed away a stranger in a strange land, yet at home among brethren.

HESTER ANN ROGERS
Her husband said, "I know that Jesus Christ has long been your all in all. Can you now tell us He is so?" She replied, "I can. He is... yes... but I cannot talk."

HANNAH MOORE - A.D. 1834
"Patty... Joy."

BILLY BRAY - A.D. 1868

On Friday, May 22, he came downstairs for the last time. To one of his old friends, a few hours before his death, who asked him if he had any fear of death, or of being lost, he said, "What? Me fear death? Me lost? Why my Saviour conquered death. If I was to go down to hell, I would shout, 'Glory! Glory!' to my blessed Jesus until I made the bottomless pit ring again. And the miserable old Satan would say, 'Billy, this is no place for thee; get thee back. Then up to heaven I should go, shouting, 'Glory! Glory! Praise the Lord!'" A little later he said, "Glory!" which was his last word.

MRS. GRIMES - A.D. 1867

"He hath wiped all tears from my eyes."

W. GREENWOOD

"All is well — very well."

WILLIAM DAWSON - A.D. 1841

(The Yorkshire Farmer)

"Let us in life, in death,
Thy steadfast truth declare."

These were the last syllables he could clearly frame. Trying to add the concluding lines of the verse, he said:

"And publish with our latest breath,
Thy love and guardian care."

Then his utterance failed, and he took up the new song with the redeemed on high.

MR. HARRISON (Tom O'Jack's Lad)
"Remember... live so as to die in the Lord.... I know that my Redeemer liveth."

MARY MOORE
"The last enemy that shall be destroyed is death."

ESTHER BROUGH - A.D. 1808
After one of her friends had prayed with her, she lifted up her hands and with great energy cried, "Victory! Victory through the blood of the Lamb!" Among her last words were, "There is light in the valley."

SUSANNA WESLEY - A.D. 1742
"My dear Saviour! Have You come to help me in my extremity at last?" Her last injunction was, "Children, as soon as I am released, sing a psalm of praise to God."

MRS. STEVENS
"Open the gates of glory! Open the gates of glory!"

ELIZABETH BATTY
"My confidence increases; I am dying."

TOM PAINE - A.D. 1809
"I would give worlds if I had them, that the 'Age of Reason' had never been published." In answer to Dr. Manley's question, "Do you then believe in the divinity of Jesus Christ?" Paine's reply and last utterance was, "I have no wish to believe on that subject."

MR. (NAME WITHHELD)

Asking his wife for a glass of water, he said: "I will not be able to get any where I am going." He drank it greedily; then looking his wife in the face, exclaimed: "Oh! Martha, Martha, you have sealed my everlasting damnation!" and died.

LUCY G. THURSTON - A.D. 1941

Her mother asked, "Whom do you love, my dear?" The dying one said, "Jesus Christ. I love Him with all my heart, with all my soul and with all my strength. Mother, I know I love Him. I do.... I do."

DR. PAYSON - A.D. 1827

"The battle's fought, the battle's fought, and the victory is won forever! I am going to bathe in an ocean of purity and benevolence and happiness to all eternity. Faith and patience, hold out."

GEORGE RUSSELL - A.D. 1895

The following words were spoken to his daughter: "I'm sweeping... through... the gates... Rosa!" (George Russell's daughter, Rosa, was author M.C. Pritchard's first wife.)

MINNIE FERGUSON - A.D. 1904

"Nothing but the plain way would have done me. Oh, happy day that fixed my choice."

SIR EDWARD COKE - A.D. 1634

"Thy kingdom come. Thy will be done!"

CHARLES ATMORE - A.D. 1826

"I have lived to die; but now I die to live. Memory and recollections are almost gone. And you see," he remarked as he held up his shrunken hand, "that I am quite in ruins! What a ruin! But, thank God, I am not dismayed; for though my heart and flesh fail, God is my portion. I scarcely dare to hope for a triumphant end, but merely an entrance into the haven of repose — that with the crew of the vessel in which St. Paul sailed, I might gain the shore on broken pieces of the ship. But God is better than all. He has promised an abundant entrance." To his weeping family he said, "Oh, do give me up! Let me go! Glory, glory, glory! Jesus! Jesus!"

DR. BEAUMONT

He expired in the pulpit while pronouncing these words:

"The while the great archangel sings,
He hides his face behind his wings,
And ranks of shining hosts around,
Fall worshipping and spread the ground."

VENERABLE BEDE - A.D. 735

Bede was occupied in dictating a translation of St. John's Gospel to an amanuensis. The young man said, "There is now but one sentence wanting." And when the scribe said, "It is now done," the dying sage replied, "It is now done." And in a few moments, he expired on the floor of his cell, in the act of prayer.

CARDINAL BEAUFORT - A.D. 1447

Cardinal Beaufort was a rich prelate in the reign of Henry VI.

Perceiving that death was at hand, he exclaimed, "Wherefore should I die, being so rich? If the whole realm would save my life, I am able either by policy to get, or by wealth to buy it! Will not death be bribed? Will money do nothing?"

MR. JONES - A.D. 1826

He perished with four other missionaries, exclaiming, "Come, Lord Jesus! Come quickly! Glory! Glory!"

A COVENANTER

Written on his prison walls on the morning of his execution, were the following last words of a Covenanter:

"My last sun has risen;
Tis far on its way.
My soul quits her prison
Ere the close of day.
Farewell hours of sorrow,
I shall know no more.
Ere day dawn tomorrow
Our union is o'er —

"A bright ray is glowing
O'er the river of death;
I fear not its flowing
With that light for my path!
Blest beam of His tracing,
O'er the gloom of the river,
Who, its horrors embracing,
Has calmed it forever!"

BELLYARMINE - A.D. 1621
"It is safest to trust in Jesus."

DR. C. J. DAVIS - A.D. 1871
A friend said to him, "You are very ill; the Lord has laid His hand upon you, but His loving arms are around you." He quickly replied, "Oh, yes, and that is enough... and that is enough... and that is enough!" He then folded his hands across his breast, saying gently, "And now I am going to sleep," and expired.

JARMAN
"All is bright, as regards the world to come. Christ is my hope, my rock! My soul is safe in Him!"

REV. ALPHONSE LA CROIX
"All is well! No doubt, no fear; perfect peace. Jesus is near!"

MARY DAWS
"What glory!"

A SCOTTISH MINISTER
Upon his deathbed, he was asked if he thought himself dying. "Really, friend," he replied, "I care not whether I am or not; for if I die, I shall be with God; and if I live He will be with me!"

DR. SCORSLEY - A.D. 1857
"I desire to depart, and to be with Christ, which is far better. But if it is His will to spare me, I trust I shall live to His glory!"

J. SHEWELL - A.D. 1800

"I am happy, happy. The enemy is not permitted to give one thrust."

MARY E. CARPENTER

Mary was an African missionary. She died while saying, "Living or dying, it's all right!"

A LITTLE HUGUENOT BOY

During the siege of Sincere, on the banks of the Loire in A.D. 1573, 500 persons died of famine. Closely encompassed by their enemies, the Huguenots — having killed and eaten the horses, mules, donkeys, and even the dogs contained in the city — were reduced to the necessity of eating not only moles, mice, rats, etc., but also parchment, leather and hoofs.

A boy of ten years old, at the point of death, seeing his parents distressed at his condition, said to them, "Wherefore weep ye thus at seeing me famish to death, Mother? I ask no bread; I know you have none. But seeing that it is God's will that I should die this death, let us be thankful for it." He then expired.

MRS. SCUDAMORE - A.D. 1800

"Dearest Lord."

DUKE OF SOMERSET - A.D. 1444

"Lord Jesus, save me!"

HARRIET SPURR

"Happy, happy, in the love of Jesus...oh, more than happy, triumphant!" In sleep, shortly before her death, she whispered these words:

"Tis but in part I know;
No mortal tongue can tell
The weight of bliss my soul shall bear
When, Lord, with Thee I dwell."

RISDEN DARRACOT

"Well, I am going from weeping friends to congratulating angels and rejoicing saints in heaven and glory. Blessed be God, all is well!"

JOHN SWAIL

"Oh, what glory! The room is full of glory!"

RACHEL FIELDING

"My God and my all! My God and my all!"

A POOR MENTALLY ILL MAN IN SCOTLAND

Up to the day of his death, he had never uttered a rational word. Yet, in his dying hour, he opened his eyes in amazement at what was revealed to his soul by the Spirit of God. He then exclaimed as follows: "I see! I see! What do I see? Three in one, and one in three, and all the three are all for me! All for me!"

VOLTAIR - A.D. 1778

Alternately praying and blaspheming, this wretched man died

crying, "Oh, Christ! Oh, Jesus Christ!"

DR. CULLEN - A.D. 1790
"I wish I had the power to write for you. I would describe how pleasant it is to die."

LITTLE SUSAN
"Weep not for me, I am going home to die no more, and I will meet you on the banks of the river... good-bye... dear... friends... I... am... going... home."

JERRY McAULEY - A.D. 1884
To one of his converts who stood at his bedside, he said, pointing toward heaven, "It's all right up there."

ESTHER CURPHEY
"Not the dark valley. There is no dark in it. Oh, praise Him! Praise Him!"

SIMEON PERKINS
"Come, Lord Jesus. Oh, that all the world...."

VARA (A Chief of the Island of Aimeo)
"I have been very wicked," he said on his deathbed, "but a great King from the other side of the skies sent His ambassadors with terms of peace. We could not tell for many years what these ambassadors wanted. At last Pomare invited all his subjects to come and take refuge under the wings of Jesus; and I was one of the first to do so. The blood of Jesus is my foundation, and I grieve that all my children do not know Him."

When asked if he was afraid to die, "No, no," was his reply. "The canoe is on the sea, the sails are spread — she is ready for the gale. I have a good pilot to guide me, and a good haven to receive me. My outside man and my inside man differ. Let the one rot till the trumpet shall sound, but let my soul wing her way to the throne of Jesus."

MISS BOOTHE
She said, "The angels say there is plenty of room up there. It's all right there." Then she waved her hand in a token of victory.

JAMES HANNINGTON - A.D. 1885
In making his way across the continent of Africa, he was taken captive by a hostile tribe. While in momentary danger of his life, he sang, "Safe in the arms of Jesus." He was condemned to death, and yet with the lofty dignity of a Christian who had lived for his God and was prepared to die for Him, he spoke a few words — a very few. "Tell the king that I die for Uganda," he said. "I have bought this road with my life."

IGNATIUS OF ANTIOCH - A.D. 107
"Let the fire and the cross, the assault of wild beasts, the breaking of bones, the cutting of limbs, the battering of the whole body in pieces... yea, and all the torments which the devil can invent, come upon me, so I may but attain to be with Christ."

RALPH SMITH
"Jesus Christ, and a convoy? Triumphant! Glorious!"

MARTIN LUTHER - A.D. 1546

His friends wanted him to take some medicine. "I am going and shall soon render up my spirit," said Luther, repeating three times, "Father, into Thy hands I commend my spirit, for Thou hast redeemed me, Thou God of truth." He then lay quite still, making no reply to the questions of those about him, until after rubbing his pulse with strengthening waters. Dr. Jones said in his ear, "Rev. Father, will you stand by Christ and the doctrines you have preached? Does it stand the agony of death?" Luther cried, "Yes, yes! A thousand times yes!" cried Luther, and turning on his side he fell asleep.

MRS. WINSLOW

"What a glorious prospect! Christ is the rock upon which my feet are placed!"

MRS. THOS. BLANCHARD - A.D. 1905

"Oh, it is glorious! Jesus is here, right here!"

BISHOP HAMBY

A while before he died, the bishop was observed to be weeping by his daughter, who sat by his couch weeping. "What is it, Father?" was the tender inquiry. "Oh, I'm so happy," was the reply. "My long, toilsome journey is nearly ended; my life work is joyfully over.... Half of my children are already safe in heaven, and I am just as sure the rest will be. Half are safe at home, and all the rest are on the way. Mother is there (referring to his wife), and in a little while I shall be there too. These lines are in my mind constantly:

"The Lord my Shepherd is,
I shall be well supplied;
Since He is mine and I am His,
What can I want beside?"

After he had descended into the river, he shouted back, "I'm in the midst of glory!"

RALPH ERSKINE - A.D. 1752
"I shall be forever a debtor to free grace. Victory! Victory!"

GUSTAVUS ADOLPHUS - A.D. 1632
At the battle of Lutzen, the king was hit in the back by a ball. He fell from his horse, saying, "I am a dead man... leave me, and only try to save your own life." While on the ground, surrounded by Croatians, they asked who he was. "I am the King of Sweden," he boldly replied, "and seal with my life's blood the Protestant religion and liberty of Germany." He then added, "Alas! my poor Queen," and as he expired cried, "My God! My God!"

A MARTYR'S ADDRESS TO HIS WIFE
"Good-bye, Mary, till morning." The next morning, as she was being put into a sack to be thrown into a pond, she handed her babe to a kind neighbour and said, "Good-bye, children... good-bye friends... I go to my husband. We will soon meet again. Christ lights the way."

MAJOR VANDELEUR
Twice he was heard to whisper, "Jesus only."

PAYSON

"The crystal city is full in view — its glories beam upon me; its breezes fan me; its odours are wafted to me; its music strikes upon me; and its spirit is breathed into my heart. Nothing separates me from it but the river of death, that now appears as a narrow rill that may be crossed at a single step when God gives me permission."

AN INDIAN CONVERT

When dying, one enquired how she felt? "Happy! Happy!" she replied. And laying her hand upon her Bible she said, "I have Christ here," and pressing it to her heart, "I have Christ here," and pointing to heaven, "and Christ there."

TINDAL - A.D. 1733

Tindal, an infidel, was originally a Protestant, then Catholic, then Protestant again. His last words were, "If there be a God, I desire that He may have mercy upon me."

EVA GREENING - A.D. 1887

(A Child of Nine Years)

While lying perfectly still and calm, she said, "I see stars!" When asked what they looked like, she said, "Bright lights, the stars of God. I see an angel!" One asked what he was like. She said, "He has on white robes." She again said, "I see angels clapping their hands around the great white throne."

SAMUEL IBBS

"Oh, what a fine throne! With someone standing with extended arms to receive me! Tis Jesus standing! I am coming presently. All is well. Jesus does all things well. Amen, amen."

DR. PRESTON - A.D. 1628
"Blessed be God, though I change my place, I shall not change my company; for I have walked with God while living, and now I go to rest with God!"

REV. THOS. COLLINS - A.D. 1864
Severe spasms in the region of the heart again beset him, during the paroxysms of which he prayed in feebly uttered words, "Father! Father! Help! Blessed Redeemer, help! Thou my friend, my life, my all, help!"

Through the whole keen conflict of suffering, he was patient, gentle and uncomplaining. In every lull of pain, or interval of relief, he became full of praise, and often exclaimed, "Glory to God! Glory to God!" He peacefully breathed his last breath in his daughter's arms.

FRANCIS QUARLES - A.D. 1644
"Oh, sweet Saviour of the world, let Thy last words upon the cross be my last words in the world: Into Thy hands, Lord, I commend my spirit. And what I cannot utter with my mouth, accept from my heart and soul."

EDWARD ADAMS
"Good-bye, Mary; good-bye, forever."

ISABELLA STRAUSTON
Though weak she was joyful, and repeated part of that beautiful hymn:

"Jesus Thy blood and righteousness,
My beauty are; my glorious dress."

"How full of the atonement that hymn is," she remarked, and added, "Yes....

"Tis Jesus first and Jesus last,
Whose Spirit shall guide me safe home,
I'll praise Him for all that is past."

Here her voice failed, and her happy spirit ascended to God.

DR. GOODWIN
"Ah! Is this dying? How have I dreaded as an enemy, this smiling friend!"

C. OBEE
"I'll meet you; I'll meet you!"

ELLEN DALBY
"My Saviour calls; I must be gone. A kiss from each before I go." A painful thrill ran through every heart. At this moment she seemed to gain fresh strength. With extraordinary strength, she embraced each one. As she threw her wasted arms around the neck of Mrs. B., she said, "The Lord bless you and comfort you. Praise my Jesus for me. Oh grace! Wonder! Mercy! All is well! Lord Jesus, I come! I come!"

JOHN OWEN
"Oh, Brother Payne, the long looked for day is come at last, in

which I shall see that glory in another manner than I have yet done!"

TOPLADY - A.D. 1778
"Sickness is no affliction; pain no curse; death no dissolution. The sky is clear. There is no cloud. Come, Lord Jesus, come quickly."

MARIANN NICHOLSON - A.D. 1867
Having commended her husband and children to God, she lifted her hands and said, "I am dying, Lord Jesus, receive my spirit. Jesus... Jesus... home... safe home."

MARY HANCOCK - A.D. 1867
"I am going to sing the song of the redeemed in heaven." Her last words were, "Happy, happy!"

REV. JESSE LEE - A.D. 1816
"Glory! Glory! Glory! Hallelujah! Jesus reigns!"

J. F. OBERLIN - A.D. 1826
"The Lord bless you, and all who are dear to you. May He be with you by day and by night."

CHARLES I - A.D. 1649
"I have a good cause, and a gracious God on my side," said he. "I go from a corruptible to an incorruptible crown, where no disturbance can take place."

MRS. JOHN EDWARDS - A.D. 1871
A little before death she exclaimed: "Angels! Spirits! Beautiful!

Many! Many! Passing! Passing! Oh! How glorious!"

JESSE APPLETON - A.D. 1819
"Glory to God in the highest. The whole earth shall be filled with His glory."

MISS HOTHAM
"I can rise to take my physic, and shall I not rise to pray?"

MERRITT CALDWELL - A.D. 1848
To his wife he said, "When you visit my grave, do not come in the shades of the evening, nor in the dark of night. These are not times to visit the grave of a Christian. But come in the morning, in the bright sunshine, and when the birds are singing." His last expressions were, "Glory to Jesus! He is my trust. He is my strength! Jesus lives. I shall live also!"

MAY BARNES (Aged Eight Years)
After repeating the Lord's prayer, she sang some hymns. Just before she died, she looked toward heaven and said, "Oh Lord, my strength and my Redeemer."

A YOUNG MAN
"Oh, drive these devils away with their chains. They will drag my soul down to hell before I die! Don't come to this hell. This is hell enough! The devils are dragging me down!"

CHARLES IX, KING OF FRANCE - A.D. 1507
It was he who gave the order for the massacre of St. Bartholomew. He died a young man. During his last hours he

said, "Oh, my nurse, my nurse! What blood, what murders, what evil councils have I followed! Oh, my God! Pardon me and have mercy on me if Thou canst. I know not what I am! What shall I do? I am lost. I see it well."

HOBBS (The Skeptic) - A.D. 1679

When drawing near the grave, notwithstanding his learning and philosophy, Hobbs asserted that he was "about to take a leap in the dark." His last words were, "I shall be glad then, to find a hole at which to creep out of the world!"

DAVID STONER

"Lord, save sinners! Save them by thousands, Lord! Subdue them, Lord! Conquer them, Lord!"

JOSEPH B. SHREWSBURY - A.D. 1849

On going to the bedside of an aged local preacher, who was nearing his end, he examined into the symptoms of the disease minutely. Having done so, before writing any prescription, he was about to give some spiritual advice, according to his most invariable practice. He just uttered with solemnity these memorable words: "The soul first, and then the body." He then sunk gently down, his head fell back, and without a struggle or a sigh, in an instant, expired.

MRS. ABBOTT

"I am ready to go! All that are ready to meet me in heaven, were they to die tonight, come and shake my hand. Hallelujah to God! I am going home to glory, and to be with my Jesus!"

SARAH A. COOKE - A.D. 1864
"Though I walk through the valley of the shadow of death, I will fear no evil."

JOHN HUNT (A Fiji Missionary)
Sobbing as if in acute distress, he cried out, "Lord, bless Fiji! Save Fiji! Thou knowest my soul has loved Fiji; my heart has travailed for Fiji!" Then clasping his friend, Calvert, by the hand, he exclaimed again, "Oh, let me pray once more for Fiji! Lord, for Christ's sake, bless Fiji; save Fiji!" Turning to his mourning wife he said, "If this be dying, praise the Lord!"

Looking up, he exclaimed, "I want strength to praise Him abundantly!" With the note of triumph, and the word "hallelujah" on his lips, he passed away.

BACON (The Sculptor) - A.D. 1799
He left the following words to be put on his tombstone: "What I was, as an artist, seemed to me to be of some importance while I lived; but what I really was as a believer in Christ Jesus, is the only thing of importance to me now."

MRS. RICHARD McMULLEN
"I have a vision. Oh glory! I see Jesus!"

THOS. LAIDMAN HODGSON - A.D. 1841
(A Missionary in South Africa)

"I see the pearly gates. They are open for me, unworthy me, and I shall enter in." A few hours later he exclaimed, "Victory! Victory! Victory! Victory through the blood of the Lamb." As his breath was failing, he began to repeat the names of some of his sainted relations. His last words were, "Hosts! Hosts! Hosts!"

MARY COOPER

Noticing that Mary's eyes were resting on a particular part of the room, and her countenance beaming, her sister asked, "Do you see something?" Mary answered, "Yes! Yes! Angels! Angels!" Her last words were, "Don't fret; all is well!"

REV. RICHARD WATSON - A.D. 1833

"I shall see God! I... I... individually. I, myself, a poor worm of the earth, shall see God!

AN OLD CHRISTIAN LADY

Her daughter Maggie had died some time before, and said when dying, "Mother, when you come to heaven, I shall be at the gate waiting for you." Now as the mother lay dying, her eldest daughter was waiting on her. "Mother," said the daughter, "shall I sing your favourite hymn?" Replied the dying saint, "Yes, 'Waiting And Watching For Me.'"

She sang the first stanza of that popular hymn. The singer was repeating the words, "Will anyone then, at the beautiful gate...." Suddenly her mother sprang up, as if she saw her beloved daughter close at hand, and exclaimed, "There's Maggie at the gate!" A moment more and she breathed her last.

JOHN HUSS (A Martyr) - A.D. 1415

"What I taught with my lips, I now seal with my blood."

A DYING INFIDEL
"Too late! Too late! Too late!"

JOHN CASSIDY
"No other name! It was a mistake... to think that any priest could get me to heaven.... But Jesus Christ can... and I think He will.... I'm happy. I'm not frightened now. Good-bye, Morris, tell... all... the poor fellows... about... the blood... cleanseth...." No more words, only a shiver, a sigh, and all was over.

AN AFRICAN CONVERT
Looking up with an expression of sweet composure, she said, "I am looking for the coming of the Lord Jesus." Observing a Christian talking to her unbelieving daughters, weeping around her bed, she remarked, "Yes, I have called them that they may see a Christian die!"

MRS. CLARKE - A.D. 1853
"There is my happy home. I shall soon be with Jesus." And then three times she repeated, "There's a balm in Gilead yet." Finally, were the words, "Blessed Jesus!"

BABYLAS (Martyr) - A.D. 250
Led to the scaffold, he said, "Return unto thy rest, oh my soul, for the Lord hath dealt bountifully with thee!" With him were executed three brothers — young men whom Babylas placed before him, giving them the precedency of martyrdom, lest their constancy might be shaken by seeing him die. As they were beheaded, he cried aloud, "Behold, I and the children, which the Lord hath given me!" Then he immediately laid

down his own neck upon the block.

MRS. MARY ROBINSON
"Christ is precious! Christ is a rock."

A. J. GORDON
"Victory!"

SIR WALTER SCOTT - A.D. 1832
"God bless you all!"

MR. MEAD
When crossing over to heaven, Mr. Mead was asked how he did? He answered, "I am going home as fast as I can, as every honest man should do when his day's work is done. I bless God that I have a home to go to."

RICHARD BAXTER - A.D. 1691
"I have pain... there is no arguing against sense... but I have peace! I have peace!"

MARGARETTA KLOPPSTOCK
"The blood of Jesus Christ cleanseth from all sin! Oh, sweet words of eternal life."

HARVEY WHITE
"Here she is, with two angels with her. They've come for me."

ELIZABETH ALLIN - A.D. 1845
Lifting her feeble arms, she faintly whispered, "Vic... vic... victory! Victory through the blood of the Lamb!" To her

weeping mother, she said, "Your Elizabeth will soon rest with her Saviour! What a Christmas I shall have! I shall be with Jesus and shall drink the wine of His Kingdom." Her life was evidently fast ebbing when she exclaimed, "Tell me, my soul, can this be death?" Then, as if conscious that the time of her departure was at hand, in holy exultation she added, "Lend, lend your wings.... I mount, I fly." A few moments later she expired, repeating that beautiful verse:

"Tis Jesus, the First and the Last,
Whose Spirit shall guide me safe home,
I'll praise Him for all that is past,
And...."

Here her voice hushed forever.

JOAN OF ARC - A.D. 1431
She died uttering the name, "Jesus!"

MRS. GIBBS - A.D. 1848
Mrs. Gibbs began reciting a portion of the hymn, "I'll praise my Maker while I've breath." Her daughter then recited the rest of the words:

"There is my house and portion fair,
My treasure and my heart are there,
And my abiding home...."

To these words, Mrs. Gibbs replied, "Yes, and the house is large enough for us all," referring to her sorrowing husband and daughter, who were both present. She added, "We may all three be there." After a pause, addressing her daughter, she exclaimed, "Oh, Sarah, He is coming! He is coming! The chariots are coming! Oh how beautiful! I never before saw anything so beautiful. I cannot describe it to you." Again she articulated, "Glory! Glory!" A few moments later she passed over to be with Jesus.

HUMBOLDT - A.D. 1835
Gazing on the sun, Humboldt exclaimed, "How bright those rays! They seem to beckon earth to heaven!"

DAVID CUTTLE - A.D. 1845
"Oh, laddie, I have seen such sights as has made my whole body tremble." A little later a friend called who asked, "Well, David, are you still a prisoner of hope?" To this he replied, "A few more minutes. A few more minutes." These were his last words.

J. ROBINSON - A.D. 1805
"I am more than a conqueror! I am more than a conqueror!"

E. HAMPON
"I can say no more, my Master is just at hand. I am waiting for His coming."

PRINCE ALBERT - A.D. 1861
"I have such sweet thoughts!"

JOHN KNOX - A.D. 1572
"By the grace of God, I am what I am. Not I but the grace of God in me, whereupon I give thanks to my God through

Jesus Christ, who has been pleased to give me the victory. Live in Christ... live in Christ, and the flesh need not fear death." With the exclamation, "Now it is come!" the reformer passed away.

REV. W. ROMAINE - A.D. 1795
"Holy! Holy! Holy! Blessed Jesus! To Thee be endless praise."

DR. HENRY - A.D. 1836
"A sweet falling of the soul on Jesus. He is now very gracious to me."

RICHARD A. BRIDIAN - A.D. 1849
"I shall soon be with Jesus."

JOHN NAYLOR - A.D. 1848
About one o'clock, he sent for one or two praying men. He could not talk much, but said, "Heaven is my home." He then exhorted all to be ready to die. His affectionate mother asked him if he was happy. He answered, "Yes," and after a short pause, added with great emphasis, "I say, yes!" In a few minutes he yielded his spirit to God, who gave it.

DR. ALEXANDER
"All my belief is this: Jesus Christ came into the world to save sinners!"

E. ARRIVE
"My Jesus hath done all things well!"

M. MAYNARD
"Christ... is... precious. The Lord is my trust."

MRS. HENRY
"If this is the 'dark' valley, it has not a dark spot in it; all is light... light. His awful holiness appears the most lovely of all His attributes. It seems as if all other glory were annihilated, and nothing left but His bare self. It will be enough. It would be a universe of glory."

MARY BISHOP - A.D. 1848
"I am now visited with a foretaste of heaven. All is well. I have a house above. Christ is mine in all His fullness. I am going to be with Him forever.

J. HENSON
"Come, Jesus, come."

PHILIP HENRY - A.D. 1696
"Oh death, where... is... thy...."

MIRABEAU - A.D. 1791
"Give me more laudanum, that I may not think of eternity, and of what is to come! I have an age of strength, but not a moment of courage."

JOHN HADISTY - A.D. 1844
"Thank God. I shall soon be home."

J. HOPKINSON
"Thank God I have done with the world!"

LAMBERT (The Martyr)
"None but Christ! NONE but Christ!"

PETER KRUSE
"All the host of heaven!"

MARY JONES
"I walk through the valley in peace." Then pointing to each one that stood around her bed, she raised her hand as if to say, "Meet me in heaven." She then folded her hands on her breast, looked up, smiled, and was gone.

IGNATIUS (Martyred By Beasts)
"Now indeed I begin to be a disciple. I weight neither visible nor invisible things, in comparison with an interest in Jesus Christ."

A YOUNG MAN
"The battle's fought, the battle's fought; but the victory is lost forever!"

BEULAH BLACKMAN
"I am so glad I have the Lord."

JENNIE GORDON
"The fiends, they come. Oh save me! They drag me down! Lost! Lost! Lost!" A moment later she said, "Bind me, ye chains of darkness! Oh, that I might cease to be, but still exist. The worm that never dies, the second death."

JOHN P. FINLEY - A.D. 1825
When one asked him how he felt, he replied, "Not the shadow of a doubt. I have Christ within, the hope of glory. That comprehends all!"

AN OLD MAN - A.D. 1883
With his last breath he uttered, "I am going to hell."

DR. HOPE - A.D. 1786
"Christ! Angels! Beautiful, magnificent, delightful! I thank God!"

ELLA GULCH
As death drew near, she said to her parents, "I am going home," and commenced singing her favourite hymn:

"O happy day, that fixed my choice,
On Thee my Saviour and my God;
Well may this glowing heart rejoice,
And tell its raptures all abroad."

"Yes," she whispered, "it was a happy day." Then putting her arms around her father's neck, whose heart seemed almost broken, she said, "Don't care for me, Father. Jesus will take care of me."

MRS. JEWETT
Mrs. Jewett suffered from cancer in the throat, and actually starved to death. She said, "I am starving to death, but in a little while I shall pluck the fruit of the tree of life." She reached out her hand as if already doing so, saying, "Sweet,

oh, how sweet!" Then dipping her hand she said, "And I shall drink of the water of life, even now.... Good-bye, for a little while."

MR. W. - A.D. 1883
On the evening of his death, Mr. N. came at ten o'clock. A friend of his was there also. As he entered the room, he felt that it was filled with an awful presence — as if it were near the regions of the damned. The dying man cried out: "Oh, God, deliver me from that awful pit!" About fifteen minutes before his death, he exclaimed: "I am in the flames! Pull me out! Pull me out!" He kept repeating this until the breath left his body. Mr. N. put his ear down to catch his departing whispers, and the last words he could hear were, "Pull me out!"

GEORGE E. DRYER - A.D. 1896
"Angels now are hovering round us." He continued to praise God, often saying under his breath, "Precious Jesus," until his soul fled from the body to realms of light.

WILLIAM FOSTER - A.D. 1887
"My heaven! Heaven! Glory!"

BISHOP OTTERBEIN
"Jesus, Jesus, I die, but Thou livest, and soon I shall live with Thee." Then turning to his friends, he continued, "The conflict is over and past. I begin to feel an unspeakable fullness of love and peace divine. Lay my head upon my pillow, and be still."

Mr. H. (A Southern Planter)

He said to his wife, who refused to allow the coachman to pray with him, "Then you will let me die and go to hell before you will suffer a Negro to pray for me!" And she did.

JOSEPH LE MOYNE - A.D. 1904

To the doctor, who was weeping, he said, "Don't cry, doctor, it is all right with my soul. My peace is made with my God." To his son, he said these words: "My boy, everything is attended to. I attended to everything while I was well — spiritual and financial. I have nothing to do now, but wait." To his granddaughter he said, "My little girl, we shall part for a little while." Then he fell asleep.

WALTER C. PALMER

"I fear no evil, for Thou art with me." After a moment's pause, he continued, "I have redeemed thee, thou art mine. When thou pass...." Then his voice failed.

MARY J. W. WIGGINS - A.D. 1897

To her pastor she said, "I will be absent from our next church meeting on earth, but I will be in heaven." To her husband and children she said, "Be good and meet me in heaven."

JOHN OXTOBY - A.D. 1829

"Oh, what have I beheld; such a sight as I possibly can't describe. There were three shining forms that stood beside me whose garments were so bright — whose countenance was so glorious — that I never saw anything to compare with them before." His dying prayer was, "Lord, save souls. Do not let them perish." Shortly after, he shouted, "Glory, glory, glory!" and was gone.

T. POTTER

A few hours before death, he was asked if he would have someone come to pray with him. To this he answered, "No, I have served the devil all my life and I have done it well; and now I will die and go to hell like a man!"

BISHOP GLOSSBRENNER

"Everything is as bright as it can be. What a blessing it is to have a Saviour at a time like this!" His last whispered words were, "My Saviour."

AMERICUS - A.D. 1874

"Please, God, make room for a little boy." These were the last words of Americus, the well-known child violinist, seven years of age, who expired very suddenly during the night of January 10, 1874, in Birston. So quietly did his spirit take its flight, that his father who occupied the same room — although hearing his son make the foregoing exclamation — thought the boy was talking in his sleep. He was horrified to find the child cold in death in the morning.

JOHN HAIME - A.D. 1784

"When my soul departs from this body, a convoy of angels will conduct me to the paradise of God."

A MERCHANT

A New York merchant who was worth 80 million dollars said with his last breath, "Poor, wretched, miserable."

LAST WORDS OF A MOTHER AND CHILD

Little Mary was an attendant of an industrial school in New York City. In her last moments she sang, "Come to Jesus," when the angels carried her to heaven. Two years later the mother died. As death drew near, she exclaimed, "Don't you hear my child singing? She is singing the same sweet song, 'Come to Jesus,' that she learned at school."

AN AGED INFIDEL

Just before he died, he summoned all his strength, rose up in his bed, and shouted, "Hell and damnation! Hell and damnation!" He then fell back, choked, strangled, and died.

MRS. C. KIRKLAND - A.D. 1864

Looking upward and eagerly raising both hands, she exclaimed in a voice of holy triumph, which no words can describe: "Oh glory! Oh glory! Oh glory!" and was gone.

MARY JANE HOWS

"Sing another hymn, for I am so happy, I must sing." A friend commenced singing, "Jesus of Nazareth passeth by." Suddenly she interrupted, "No! No! Not that!" She exclaimed, "Jesus is not passing by, He is here in my room... in my soul.... Sing, 'Ring the bells of heaven.'"

When asked if she was tired, she replied, "Oh, no. I am crossing the river, but the water is not deep. I can feel the bottom, and like David, I can walk through the valley of the shadow of death. It is the way home to my Father's house above."

A little while after she said to her mother, "Hark, Mother! Hark! They're singing! Oh, such singing! I see angels. I shall have a harp of gold, and oh, won't I strike it loud when I reach the other side!" Her last words were, "Jesus! Jesus! My... precious... Jesus."

JOHN THORNTON - A.D. 1790
Someone asked him whether he was now happy. "Yes," he said, "Happy in Jesus. All things are as well as they can be!" The last words he was able to articulate were, "Precious, precious...."

JACOB BOEHME - A.D. 1624
On November 18, 1624, early in the morning, he asked his son Tobia, "Do you hear the excellent music?" He replied, "No." He then said to his son, "Open the door that it may be better heard." At six o'clock, he exclaimed, "Now, I go hence to Paradise," sighed deeply and expired.

BISHOP BEDELL - A.D. 1641
"Oh, Lord, I have waited for Thy salvation! I know whom I have believed, and am persuaded that He is able to keep that which I have committed to Him against that day."

BISHOP HAVEN - A.D. 1880
"There is no river here! All is beautiful."

MR. SMITH - A.D. 1905
"I'm going home to die no more."

DR. BELLAMY - A.D. 1790

When dying he was much depressed. "Alas!" he said, "that I, who have laboured for others, myself should be a castaway!" A friend present said to him, "If God should send you to hell, dear Brother, what would you do there?" "I would tell them there forever, that Jesus is precious," replied the dying saint.

BOETON

"My friend, you think I am in pain; you are not mistaken. I do suffer, but He who is with me, and for whom I suffer, gives me strength to bear my agony with joy!"

REV. T. COOKE

When asked by a friend if God were now his support, he replied, "Oh, yes, it cannot be otherwise. It cannot be that my God should now forsake me. He is bound to me by a thousand indissoluble ties!"

J. G. BELLETT - A.D. 1864

Clasping his thin hands together, while tears flowed down his face, he said, "My precious, Lord Jesus, Thou knowest how fully I can say with Paul, 'To depart and to be with Thee is far better.' Oh, how far better! I do long for it! They come and talk to me of the crown of glory. I bid them cease. Of the glories of heaven, I bid them stop. I am not wanting crowns. I have Himself... Himself! I am going to be with Himself! Ah, with the Man of Sychar; with Him who stayed to call Zaccheus; with the Man of John VIII; with the Man who hung upon the cross; with the Man who died! Oh, to be with Him before the glories, the crowns, or the kingdoms appear! It is wonderful! Wonderful! With the Man of Sychar alone, the Man of the gate of the city of Nain; and I am going to be with Him forever. Exchange this sad, sad scene, which cast Him out, for His presence! Oh, the Man of Sychar!"

RICHARD CROMWELL - A.D. 1712
"Live in love. I am going to the God of love."

BISHOP BEVERIDGE - A.D. 1707
His memory completely failed when he was upon his deathbed. Even his most intimate friends and his loving wife were unrecognized. "Well," said one standing by his bedside, "Bishop Beveridge, do you know Jesus Christ?" The dying man replied, "Oh, yes. I have known Him these 40 years. Precious Saviour. He is my only hope!"

RABBI BEN ZACCHAI
"There are two ways before me: the one to hell, the other to Paradise. And I know not into which they are carrying me. Shall I not weep?"

HENRY BIRCH
"In the highest heights, and then...."

BILNEY - A.D. 1530
"Jesus, I believe!"

CLEMENT BROWN
He pointed with his finger, and said, "I see, one, two, three, four, five angels waiting their commission." He then counted them again, and said, "They are four, only four. I see them as

plainly as I see you, Hester. How I wish you could see them! They are splendidly robed in white." Lifting up both hands, he said, "Angels beckon me away, and Jesus bids me come. Come, Lord Jesus, come quickly."

FRANCIS MOORE - A.D. 1825
To her brother, Bishop McKendree, she said, "Even so, come, Lord Jesus!" Then with her hands feebly raised, she responded, "So be it! Glory! Oh, the beauty!" These were her last words.

EDWARD BICKERSTETH - A.D. 1850
"I have no other ground of confidence than the blood of Jesus. Christ first, Christ last, Christ all in all."

CALIPH ABD-ER-RHAMAN - A.D. 961
"50 years have passed away since first I was caliph. Riches, honour, pleasure... I have enjoyed all. In this long period of seeming happiness, I have numbered the days on which I have been happy. They amount to 14."

N. R. COBB
"Nothing can equal my enjoyment in the near prospect of heaven. My hope in Christ is worth infinitely more than all other things. The blood of Christ. The blood of Christ... none but Christ!"

ROBERT BOLTON - A.D. 1631
"Oh, when will this good hour come? When shall I be dissolved? When shall I be with Christ?"

HELENA FREDERIC
"Oh, how beautiful."

PUNCH (A Negro Preacher)
On the Sabbath morning, he told me he should die that day. He addressed affecting words to the people, who crowded around his dying bed. The burden of his remarks — the theme of his soul — was, "Now, Lord, lettest Thou Thy servant depart in peace." He applied these words to himself, and continued his addresses to the last moment; and death gently stole his spirit away while saying, "Let Thy servant depart in peace... let... let... le...!"

JOHN CHAPPELL
"I can scarcely speak; my breath is almost gone. Oh, I wish I could talk of the mercies of my blessed Redeemer!"

J. BROWN
Putting out his hand, he was asked, "What are you reaching?" He whispered, "A kingdom," and passed away.

AYMOND DE LAVRY - A.D. 1555
When this Protestant minister of Bordeaux was at the stake, he cried out, "Oh, Lord, make haste to help me! Tarry not. Despise not the work of Thy hands." And to those standing around, who aforetime had been his hearers, he said, "My friends, I exhort you to study and learn the Gospel, for the Word of God abideth forever. Labour to know the will of God; and fear not them that kill the body, but have no power over the soul." The executioner then strangled him, and burnt his body.

CAESAR BORGIA - A.D. 1507

"I have provided, in the course of my life, for everything except death. And now, alas! I am to die, although entirely unprepared."

BISHOP McKENDREE

The last words that trembled upon his lips were, "All is well."

W. DAY

The dying saint, profusely weeping, cried, "Oh, when shall I behold Christ as He is, and cast myself at His feet? The world has shown me its favours, and taken them away again. I have enjoyed many tokens of the loving kindness of God, and I have at other times been stripped of what I most valued; but, oh, my God, my Redeemer, Thou hast never failed me!"

CECIL'S MOTHER - A.D. 1777

One asked, "Are you afraid to die?" She answered, "No! No!" Another question was then asked, "Does the uncertainty of another state give you no concern?" She replied, "God has said, 'Fear not; when thou passest through the waters I will be with thee, and through the rivers, they shall not overflow thee.'"

MICHAEL BRUCE - A.D. 1767

"Why should not a man be cheerful on the verge of heaven?"

PHILIP DODDRIDGE - A.D. 1751

"Though I have not felt all the rapturous joy, which I have sometimes done, yet I am sure that the Lord is my God; and I have a cheerful, well-grounded hope, through the Redeemer, of being received to His everlasting mercy and glory."

ED BURK'S SON
He died repeating the lines of Milton:

"His praise ye winds that from four quarters blow,
Breathe soft or loud; and wave your tops, ye pines,
With every plant, in sign of worship, wave!"

JOHN DODD
"I am not afraid to look death in the face. I can say, 'Death where is thy sting?' Death cannot hurt me!"

MARTIN BRAUN - A.D. 1906
In the prime of life, and surrounded by comforts and all things necessary to make life happy, he met with an accident which bruised and mangled his body, and eventually caused his translation. During his short sickness, he was lifted above this world and pain, rejoiced in God, had a vision of angels, and departed uttering the words, "How loving, how good is God!"

HENRY TOWNLEY
"My body is full of pain; but my soul is full of glory."

REV. WILLIAM DAWSON
"Let us in life, in death, Thy steadfast truth declare."

MRS. DOBINSON
"My trust is in a precious Christ."

DAVID FREDERICK STRAUSS

"In the enormous machinery of the universe, amid the incessant whirl and hiss of the jagged iron wheels, amid the deafening crash of its ponderous stamps and hammers, in the midst of this whole terrific commotion, man—a helpless and defenceless creature—finds himself placed not secure for a moment on an imprudent motion. A wheel may seize and rend him, or a hammer crush him to powder. This sense of abandonment is something awful."

J. DUCKWORTH - A.D. 1817

"The Lord is my joy, my hope, my treasure. He is my comfort and my delight. Oh, Thou great Omnipotent, come down and seize me for Thine own! Oh, my precious, my precious Saviour!"

ARISTOTLE

"In pollution I entered the world. Anxiously I have lived in it; miserably do I depart from it. Oh, Thou cause of causes, have mercy upon me."

HENRY BLUNT

When Henry Blunt was dying, the doctor said to him, "Sir, you are drawing near the grave; and I think if you have any accounts to settle, you had better settle them." Mr. Blunt replied, "I have no accounts to settle. I owe nothing to man, and my Saviour has paid all my debts to God."

DAVID LIVINGSTONE - A.D. 1873

His last words were written in his diary: "All I can add in my loneliness is, may heaven's richest blessing come down on everyone — American, English, Turk—who will help to heal this open sore of the world."

MRS. WM. NEWMAN - A.D. 1910

Shortly before she died, she spoke of her beloved daughter and said, "Mary is in a beautiful place. Oh, heaven is a beautiful place! I am going home. It is so easy to die. Oh, it is so easy to die!"

ALBERT THE GOOD (Husband of Queen Victoria)

"I have had wealth, and rank, and power, and I thank God for them; but if these were all, I should now be poor indeed!" Then as his spirit was passing away, he whispered these words:

"Rock of Ages, cleft for me,
Let me hide myself in thee!"

A LITTLE BOY

A little boy lay dying. A short time before, his mamma had died. His father sat by the bedside weeping. Stretching out his hand, the little one said, "Good-bye, Papa. Mamma has come for me tonight! Don't cry, Papa. We'll all meet again in the morning!"

OLYMPHIA MORATA

"I distinctly behold a place, filled with ineffable light."

REV. A. B. VANCAMP - A.D. 1905 (Missionary of China)
The following messages were dictated by our brother shortly
before he died:

"Dear Mother: Have gone to be with Jesus. Weep not for me.
We shall meet again. Mother, your prayers, your humility, your
love, changed my hell to heaven. Father calls... I'm away."

"Dear Father: Farewell. I'm the first to lay the burden down."

"Morley, my beloved brother: We lived together in love. I'll
meet you at the gathering at the river."

"Sister Cora: Cora, toil on. Thy path will be hard sometimes,
but I know you will overcome, and enter into His love."

"Louva: I've gladly said I'd give up my life for your salvation.
Meet me in the city of life, where we shall part no more."

"Sister Louisa: I'll be looking for you."

"Mr. Horner: I shall work no more; now will be praising Jesus
throughout eternity."

"Miss Burke, Egypt: I told you seven years gone by, I'd go to
heaven from China. Farewell, sister."

"Conference Fellows: My voice hushes on the evening air to
breathe the full life of the immortality of my God. I say to you
over again, it was God's voice leading me to China. Farewell."

HETTIE KERR - A.D. 1910
Just before she died, Hettie was asked if she was afraid to meet death. Her answer was, "Oh, no." At another time, she said, "There is one thing I want you to remember: It's all right!"

MRS. ROLLINS - A.D. 1908
Putting up her hand, she asked her husband, "Where am I going?" He replied, "To heaven." To which she responded, "Praise God!"

MRS. JANET NORVIL KILMOUR - A.D. 1882
"Oh, my Father, it is a fine thing to be over there.

DR. SAMUEL KENNEDY - A.D. 1911
The following words were found in his wallet on December 10, 1911, shortly after he died:

"Oh change! Stupendous change!
There lies the soulless clod,
The light eternal breaks,
The new immortal wakes,
Wakes with his God!"

ALICE ELYEA
As death drew near, she requested those who stood there to sing some hymns. As they were about to do so, she stopped them, saying, "Stop! The angels are singing! Don't sing. The angels are singing now!" Looking up, she said, "Oh, I see Jesus!" and was gone.

JOHNNY REYNOLDS
Johnny, a little boy, only three years old, said just before he died, "Mamma, don't cry. Jesus loves Johnny."

JOHN HOLLAND
The day before he died, he called for his Bible, saying, "Come, oh, come. Death approaches. Let us gather some flowers to comfort this hour." After some comments made on the Scripture, he exclaimed, "Oh, stop your reading! What brightness is this I see? Have you lighted up any candles?" Mr. Leigh answered, "No, it is the sunshine." "Sunshine!" he said, "It is my Saviour's shine."

"Now, farewell world; welcome heaven. The Daystar from on high hath visited my heart. I feel His mercy. I see His majesty. Whether in the body, or out of the body, I cannot tell. God knoweth. But I see things that are unutterable." Thus ravished in spirit, he roamed toward heaven. With a cheerful look and a low, soft voice, he said something just before his departure, but it could not be understood.

ELIZABETH CAIRN - A.D. 1906
"I did not think that it took so long to die. Glory! Glory! Glory! Tell the friends to meet me in heaven; and tell them at the Guardian office that all is well."

MRS. CYRENA CLARKE - A.D. 1893
"I do! I do! I do love Jesus!" She repeated again, "I do! I do! I do love Jesus!" And again, "I do! I do! I do love Jesus!" These words were uttered just as her happy spirit was leaving the body.

PRESIDENT McKINLEY

The president, who was shot by an assassin, said with his last breath, "Not as I will; but as God wills."

CONVERTED HEATHEN CHILD

Coming to the gates of death, it was exclaimed, "After this, heaven!"

DR. GROSVENOR

"I will smile on death, if Jesus will smile on me."

JOHN GAMBLE

The last Sunday that he lived on earth, he was visited by the Rev. Mr. Richardson. "Little John," who was but very young, gathered all his money and gave it to him for the missionaries. Three times he called his beloved pastor back and kissed him, and told him to meet him in heaven. Tears flowed down the pastor's face as he said, "I will." Early the next morning he told his parents that he was going to Jesus, and in two hours passed sweetly away.

GENERAL BOOTH - A.D. 1912

His last message to Salvationists throughout the world was, "His promises, they are sure, they are sure, if you will only believe." His last words were addressed to his son: "Don't worry; let me die. I want to go to heaven!"

ASA McINTOSH - A.D. 1913

His words to a fellow worker were, "I am well prepared to go. The only desire I have to live is that I might win a few more souls for Jesus." When told by his wife that he could not live, he said, "Everything is all right; it will soon all be over. Be true to God... go on... go on... be true... be true to Jesus!" In his delirium, he was constantly exhorting sinners to come to Jesus, and his fellow workers to "get to business and be true to God."

CATHERINE BOOTH - A.D. 1890

"The waters are rising, but so am I. I am not going under, but over. Don't be concerned about your dying; only go on living well, and the dying will be all right." Her last words were spoken to the General: "Till the day breaks and the shadows flee away...."

BLUMHARDT

"Light breaks in. Hallelujah!"

DR. WAKLEY

A few hours before his exit, he was asked, "What shall we say to your brethren in the ministry from you?" He answered:

"Preach the Word; be instant in season, out of season. Reprove, rebuke, exhort, with all long-suffering and doctrine." (He repeated the words, "with all long-suffering" three times.) After a moment's rest, he added, "Tell them what Peter says, 'If any man speak, let him speak as the oracles of God; if any man minister, let him do it as of the ability which God giveth, that God in all things may be glorified, through Jesus Christ, to Whom be praise and dominion forever and ever.' Amen."

After a moment's rest, while panting for breath, he added, "Tell them to preach the old Gospel. We want no new one. The old Gospel is to save the world. It can't be improved. One might as well attempt to improve a ray of sunshine while vivifying a flower. The grand old Gospel forever!" After a short pause to take a breath, he said, "Tell them to go where they are sent."

Speaking of his whole case — all the interests involved in his demise — he said, "I leave all with God. I want it distinctly understood. I do so without any fear, without any cowardice, without any alarm. I do it with the boldness of an old soldier, and with the calmness of a saint."

He continued, "They will inquire in the morning, 'Is Brother Wakely dead?' Dead! No! Tell them he is better, and alive forevermore." I said, "Yes, and a higher and nobler life." He replied, "Wonderfully enlarged! Oh, wonderfully enlarged!"

Here are some more wise quotes spoken by this great man of God:

"Let me have a little plot in the quiet cemetery, and let me sleep there until the great rising day."

"I know the old ship. The Pilot knows me well. He will take me safe into port. Heavenly breezes already fan my cheeks."

"I shall not be a stranger in heaven. I am well known up there."

"Like Bunyan, I see a great multitude with white robes, and I long to be with them. To depart and be with Christ is far better."

"When you go to the grave, don't go weeping. Death hath no sting. The grave hath no terror. Eternity hath no darkness. Sing at my funeral: 'Rejoice for a brother deceased; our loss is his gain.' For many years neither death nor the grave had any terrors for me."

"Hark! Hark! Hear ye not the song? Victory is ours. There is great rejoicing in heaven. Roll open, ye golden gates, and let my car go through! I must wait until the death angel descends."

A. F. HERMAN - A.D. 1895
Throwing up his hands, he waved them and said, "Go on angels, I am coming! Go on angels, I am coming!"

CROMWELL
"The devil is ready to seduce us; and I am seduced."

REV. DAVID NELSON - A.D. 1844
"My Master calls... I am going home. It is well."

HATTIE BUFORD - A.D. 1865
This little girl died in 1865, when only six years old. She was the child of Major-General John Buford. She was taught to repeat the Lord's prayer every night. As the child lay on her dying bed, and the hour of her departure was drawing near,

she all of a sudden opened her soft blue eyes, and looking confidently into her mother's face, said, "Mamma, I forgot to say my prayers!" Summoning what strength she had left, she clasped her little white hands together and, like a little angel, prayed thus:

"Now I lay me down to sleep,
I pray Thee, Lord, my soul to keep;
If I should die before I wake,
I pray, Thee, Lord, my soul to take."

When the prayer was finished, she never spoke again.

MABEL BLACK - A.D. 1906
During the intermission of pains, which were very severe, she constantly sang:

"It's the old-time religion, and it's good enough for me."

STEWART D. GEDDES - A.D. 1907
"I see Jesus. I see Him hanging on the cross for me. I see the print of the nails in His hands. Oh, glory, he saves me now!" After exhorting and sending messages to unsaved ones, he turned to his brother and said, "David, if I had listened to your exhortations I would not have been here now," meaning God would not have used this severe means. Later, he exclaimed, "I am going sweeping through the gates. Tell Brother Shields I am going home to heaven. Tell him Jesus sweetly saves me now." Later he repeated the words:

"Jesus, lover of my soul,
Let me to Thy bosom fly...."

And then when he said, "Oh, Jesus, take me home," the end soon came.

PRESIDENT EDWARDS - A.D. 1758

After settling all his worldly affairs, and bidding adieu to his family, he turned around saying, "Now, where is Jesus of Nazareth, my never failing Friend?" and fell asleep.

ROBERT A. TWIDDY - A.D. 1907

On the Friday previous to his death, while Sister Baker was calling upon him, and praying, God's Spirit came on him and he laughed, shouted and praised the Lord. Tears of joy streamed down his cheeks. On Saturday, about midnight, he exclaimed, "The best of all is, God is with us." An hour or two after, he said, "It's all right." From this he lapsed into unconsciousness, and soon was in the presence of the Lord.

JOHN HOLDEN - A.D. 1906

"I have no doubts. Christ is present and precious."

EMPEROR ADRIAN

"Ah, my poor soul! Whither art thou going?"

WILLIAM RUSSELL - A.D. 1897

"I see Jesus. He is coming to receive me."

ETHEL MOORE - A.D. 1907

She had no fear of death and never murmured during her illness, but wept and prayed over lost sinners, especially those in her home. With loving words for her dear ones who watched her slowly fading, she soothed their grief, bade them all good-bye, and said she was going. Just as her spirit was departing she had a glimpse of future glory and exclaimed, "Beautiful! Abbey ought to see it. Oh, so beautiful!" Someone gave her a drink of water, to which she replied, "You ought not to have done it, for I was just entering heaven. It is such a beautiful place!"

MRS. JACKSON - A.D. 1906

When asked if she had any message to send to Mr. Bradford, she replied, "Tell him that I died happy in the Lord!"

BLOOM

"Lord Jesus, come."

MRS. T. HOLLINGSHEAD - A.D. 1907

As the testimony meeting was entered into, she arose and gave her testimony, which was somewhat like this: "I know I am saved." She spoke about the precious blood of Jesus, and then said, "Thank God!" With this note of praise she fell over, asleep in Jesus. At first we thought she was only prostrated from the exuberance of her joy, but the fears of those near by were aroused. When her husband and family were called, we learned she had been subject to fainting spells. We carried her down to her home and a doctor was summoned, but the lamp of this life had already gone out.

SIR THOMAS SCOTT

"Until this moment I thought there was neither a God nor a hell. Now I know and feel that there are both, and I am doomed to perdition by the just judgment of the Almighty."

LOUIS McGUIRE - A.D. 1906

Though having hardly strength enough to speak above a whisper, yet about half an hour before he died, he sang aloud the praise of God. Then he clapped his hands and exclaimed, "I hear them playing their harps. I shall soon play one too." His last words were, "Praise the Lord! Amen."

GRANDMA SHEARS

"It is bright over the river. Oh, so bright over there."

MRS. BIRKS - A.D. 1906

To her pastor she said, "Preach Christ. Plead with sinners."

REV. O. R. LAMBLY - A.D. 1905

"Father, take me home."

CHRISTINA ROSIN JOHNSON - A.D. 1907

In the evening, she complained of rheumatism in her body, and not feeling well. The family awoke at midnight as she began singing, "Praise God, the victory is won." She prayed several times during the night and praised God for a clean heart. A few hours before she passed away, she prayed with uncommon strength for everybody in the house and her husband. Her last words were, "Glory! Glory! Glory!"

MRS. D. L. RANNEY

"It is all light now. The dread of suffering is gone. My blessed Saviour has given me the victory. I am ready and waiting to go. I leave you all!"

MRS. T. McKEE - A.D. 1906

Her last words to her husband were, "Mind your soul. Prepare to meet me in heaven! Praise God, I have neither doubt nor fear."

CHARLES SINCLAIR - A.D. 1907

At his request we sang, "He died because He loved me so." With much difficulty, he said these words:

"And if our fellowship below
In Jesus be so sweet,
What heights of rapture shall we know
When round His throne we meet."

After much suffering, he sweetly passed away — leaving a blessed assurance to his sorrowing friends that he had gone to worship God in the upper sanctuary where prayer is lost in endless praise. His last words were, "Jesus, Thy kingdom come."

FATHER EGIDIS

"Oh, good Jesus, Thy wounds are my merits. Yes, mine, mine. Oh, Jesus!"

NENDER

"Let us go home. Good-night!"

A LITTLE GIRL

A little girl was dying. She asked her mother to bring her mission box. Once more she took the pennies she had been saving in her weak hand, and then putting them back into the box, she gave it to her mother and whispered, "See that Jesus gets it all." Then she slipped away to glory.

MRS. THOS. WETHERELL - A.D. 1907

"I'll go every step of the way. I'll go every step of the way! Hallelujah!"

MRS. SPOFFORD - A.D. 1906

Her last words were, "Safe in the arms of Jesus."

GAMBATTA

"I am lost! I am lost!"

NATUATWEES

He was an able Indian ruler. Calling his warriors and counsellors around him, he uttered as his last request, "That the Delawares should hear and believe the Word of God." He then called Zlisberger, the faithful missionary, and begged him to explain more of the things of God. And while the latter spoke in strong emotion, the chieftain breathed his last breath.

RICHARD CECILA - A.D. 1810

"'None but Christ! None but Christ!' So said dying Lambert at the stake; and so under all circumstances, and with all his heart, says Richard Cecila."

WILLIAM PITT - A.D. 1778
"I have, like other men, neglected prayer too much to have any ground of hope that it can be efficacious on a deathbed. I throw myself on the mercy of God through the merits of Christ."

JULIUS PALMER
While at the stake, he spoke with earnest conviction. "God's Holy Spirit certifieth to our spirit, that He hath even now prepared a sweet supper in heaven for His sake, who suffered for us." In the end, moving his charred lips, he uttered the words, "Sweet Jesus!" and fell asleep until the morning of the resurrection.

RUTHERFORD - A.D. 1661
"If He slay me ten thousand times ten thousand times, I'll trust! Oh, for arms to embrace Him! Oh, for a well-tuned harp!"

ANNE ROBERTS - A.D. 1799
"Great peace have they that love Thy law—peace and joy through believing."

JOHN PHILPOT (A Martyr) - A.D. 1555
"I will pay my vows in thee, oh Smithfield!"

DR. OLIVER - A.D. 1764
He was a zealous unbeliever until shortly before his death. When dying, he said, "Oh, that I could undo the mischief that I have done! I was more ardent to poison men with infidel

principles than any Christian is to spread the doctrines of Christ."

THOMAS RUTHERFORD - A.D. 1771

"He has indeed ever been to me a precious Christ, and now I feel Him to be my rock, my strength, my rest, my hope, my joy, my all in all."

REV. FRANCIS BRAZEE

"They sing! The angels sing!"

REV. JOHN DOEL

"I am not afraid to look death in the face."

WHITEFIELD - A.D. 1770

"Lord Jesus, I am weary in Thy work, but not of Thy work. If I have not yet finished my course, let me go and speak for Thee once more in the fields, and seal the truth, and come home to die." Then he uttered, "I had rather wear out, than rust out." Suddenly he ran to the window, panting for breath, while saying, "I'm dying," and almost immediately breathed his last in his chair.

WILLIAM

"Glory be to God. I shall get the better of Satan. Glory be to Massa Jesus, I shall conquer him (Satan)!" One said, "Brother Will, is your soul happy in Massa Jesus?" He answered, "Yes," and fell asleep in Jesus.

WILLIAM LORD RUSSELL - A.D. 1683

"I think this is the happiest time of my life, though others may look on it as the saddest!"

FRANCIS SPIRA

"My sin is greater than the mercy of God. I have denied Christ, voluntarily. I feel that He holds to me no hope."

SAMUEL JOHNSTON

"Believe a dying man. Nothing but salvation in Christ can comfort you when you come to die."

SIR THOMAS SMITH - A.D. 1577

"It is a matter of lamentation, that men know not to what end they were born into the world until they are ready to go out of it."

T. C. RUSHFORD - A.D. 1808

"I shall soon be at rest. My dear Redeemer. My dear Redeemer!"

R. TREWARRAS (King's Pilot)

"I am lying off and on, waiting for the signal. I lie well, and should a storm arise and carry away all the canvass, I could send it in under bare poles. Yes, my Saviour will not leave me now."

DR. SIMPSON

"What art thou? I am not afraid of thee. Thou art a vanquished enemy through the blood of the cross."

SAUNDERS (Martyr)
"Welcome the cross of Christ; welcome everlasting life."

CHAS. WESLEY - A.D. 1788
"I shall be satisfied with Thy likeness. Satisfied... satisfied... satisfied!"

JOHN ARTHUR LYTH
"I shall soon be with Jesus. Perhaps I am too anxious. Can this be death? Why it is better than living! Tell them that I die happy in Jesus."

WILMOT (An Infidel) - A.D. 1680
When dying, Wilmot laid his emaciated hand upon the Bible and exclaimed solemnly, "The only objection against this book is — a bad life."

DR. SANDERSON - A.D. 1663
"My heart is fixed, oh God. My heart is fixed where true joy is to be found!"

JAMES WILSON - A.D. 1860
"There is no darkness in the valley; it is all bright. I will fear no evil, for Thou art with me!"

BARON BUNSEN
"With all feebleness and imperfection, I have ever lived, striven after and willed the best and noblest only. But the best and highest is to have known Jesus Christ. It is sweet to die."

JOHN BUNYAN

"We shall meet e'er long, to sing the new song, and remain happy forever in a world without end. Take me, for I come to Thee."

MISS A. ROSE STUBES

"Jesus! Jesus! Oh, what would I do without Him now! Almost home, home; my mansion is all ready."

REV. JOHN WARBURTON

"Oh, what a blaze and e' shout there will be when old John gets to heaven!"

MRS. LEWIS - A.D. 1906

Her last hours on earth proved a fitting close to such a devoted and Christ-like life, and furnished a complete refutation to the Oslerin theory (that the dying do not see visions of a better world). While relatives stood around, her face became lighted up with a radiance not of this world, as she said, "I cannot tell you how beautiful it is over there." Her last words were, "I am redeemed."

REV. PHILIP HECK

"Oh! How beautiful! The opening heavens around me shine!"

WILLIAM WHEELER

"I am coming! I am coming!"

ARCHBISHOP SHARPE - A.D. 1714

"I shall be happy!"

SIR HENRY VANE - A.D. 1662

"Blessed be the Lord that I have kept a conscience void of offence unto this day. I bless the Lord that I have not deserted the righteous cause for which I suffer."

TYNDAL - A.D. 1536

"Lord, open the King of England's eyes!"

TASSO - A.D. 1595

"Into Thy hand, oh Lord."

BISHOP PIERCE

"Rest, happiness, and peace forever."

JACOB BORHME

"Now, I go home into paradise."

TANKERFIELD (A Martyr)

A certain knight went up to him and said gently, "Good brother, be strong in Christ!" Tankerfield replied, "Oh, sir, I thank you. I am so, I thank God."

MRS. HANNAH WOOD

"I shall see Him as He is; I shall be forever near Him and behold His face. My eyes shall behold Him. I shall see Him for myself and not another. Blessed be God!"

LORD TEIGNMOUTH - A.D. 1834

"I have no hope but in Christ Jesus; in His sacrifice, in His blood."

MARTHA McCRACKIN
"How bright the room. How full of angels!"

THOMAS HUDSON (A Martyr)
When the flames were rising about him, he slipped from under the chain that held his body to the stake and, falling on his knees amidst the burning pile, his spirit wrestled with God. The martyr arose and exclaimed, "Now I thank God, I am strong, and care not what man can do unto me!"

REV. JOHN CARTER
"I am packed up and ready to go. I am waiting for the Lord to call me."

W. WHITBY
"Who's there? What's that? Angels are coming for me."

THOMAS SCOTT
"I have done with darkness forever."

MRS. VAUGHAN
A friend by her bedside said to her:

*"Jesus can make a dying bed
Feel soft as downy pillows are."*

Mrs. Vaughan quickly replied:

*"Whilst on His breast I lean my head,
And breathe my life out sweetly there."*

MOTHER MARGARET PRIOR

"Eternity rolls up before me like a sea of glory, and so near. Oh, that blessed company of redeemed sinners, and the glorious Jesus! What a Saviour; and He is mine. Oh, what a speck of time is the longest life to prepare for that blessed world."

HUGH GROTIUS

"Alas! I have spent my life in labouriously doing nothing. I would give all my learning and honour for the plain integrity of John Urick." (Urick was a poor, but very pious man.)

REV. SAMUEL BIBBINS

"The storm of life has at length blown over. The last tornado has passed by. The victory is gained and heaven is mine. Sweet haven of rest — it is mine. Then I shall see the martyrs, the apostles and confessors. Best and most of all, then I shall see Jesus!"

BENJAMIN T. HUNTER

"Brother, tell my dear wife to prepare herself to meet me in heaven, and the rest of the family also!"

SAMUEL COOK

"I have no desire to get better — would rather depart and be with Christ."

LIZZIE W. O'NEIL

"The Lord is good; I am going home to Him."

PRESIDENT ROBERT SIMPSON

"I shall go to the gates of heaven as the poor, wretched, ruined Robert Simpson, saved by sovereign grace. When I begin to tell my tale, all of the harps of heaven will be silent; all the angels will be as still as statues. I am sure they will. I am going home. Pray for me."

MRS. CICELY ORMES (A Martyr)

"Welcome, thou cross of Christ!" After the fire was kindled, she said, "My soul doth magnify the Lord, and my spirit doth rejoice in God my Saviour."

MRS. AARON SMITH

"I am happy, very happy."

JOHN EVENS

"Oh, glorious hope!"

REV. SAMUEL PIERCE

"Yes, I taste its sweetness and enjoy its fullness, with all the gloom of a deathbed before me. And far rather would I be the poor, emaciated creature that I am, than to be an emperor, with every earthly good about him, but without God."

REV. P. CORL

"Oh, I see such a fullness in Christ as I never saw before. Tell the people I am trusting in a full salvation."

S. G. BANGS

"The sun is setting; mine is rising. I go from this bed to a crown. Farewell."

REV. C. R. KESSLER

"What a blessed Sabbath has dawned on me."

THOMAS GOLDBY

"Take away the whiskey. I promised mother I'd never drink, and I won't break my word." These were his last words, spoken after he had been mortally wounded, and a glass of liquor was pressed to his lips.

REV. D. S. MONTGOMERY

I am on the borderland. All is well; all is well. Is this death? If this be death, then it is pleasant to die."

SHOEBLACK JIM

"The next time I sing will be when Jesus folds me in His arms."

REV. HENRY HARVEY

"Oh welcome, welcome death! The conflict is over."

JANE B.

A young girl, thirteen years of age, lay dying. Lifting her eyes toward the ceiling, she said softly, "Lift me higher! Lift me higher!" Her parents raised her up with pillows, but she faintly said, "No, not that, but there!" again looking earnestly toward heaven, whither her happy soul flew a few moments later. On her tombstone is carved: "Jane B— , lifted higher."

ROSE

A boy, employed in Barrow dockyard, was fearfully mangled by an engine. During the three hours which elapsed before death ended his sufferings, he repeatedly sang verses of the hymn, "Jesus, lover of my soul."

REV. Q. DICKENS

"My soul now enjoys such sweet communion with Him, that I would not give it for the whole world. Glory to Jesus!"

A LITTLE BOY

This child, who had listened to the preaching of George Whitfield and whose heart had been deeply moved by the sweet story of the cross from the lips of the eloquent evangelist, lay upon his dying bed. During a momentary pause in his sufferings, when his end was near, he stretched his hands upwards and cried, "Let me go to Mr. Whitfield's God!"

GRIFFITH JONES

"Oh, how wonderful is the love of God to me. Blessed be God! His comforts fill my soul!"

D. L. MOODY

"Earth recedes; heaven opens before me!"

A CHINESE CONVERT

"The grace of God is sufficient!"

REV. WILFRED FLOWER - A.D. 1905

Within an hour or two of his release, he joined with solemn

emphasis in the words, "These are they which came out of great tribulation, and have washed their robes and made them white in the blood of the Lamb. Therefore, are they before the throne of God and serve Him day and night in His temple." When the quotation was finished, he fervently uttered these words: "Praise be to God! Blessed be His name!" and then fell into a painless sleep in which he gently passed away.

THOMAS HOOKER
It was said to him when dying, "Brother, you are going to receive the reward of your labours." He replied, "I am going to receive mercy."

REV. JACOB DOERKSEN
"It is not death to leave this world and then with the brotherhood on high be at home with God."

DR. MASON GOOD - A.D. 1827
Because of his impaired hearing, his friend, Mr. Russell, called to him in a loud tone of voice, "Behold the Lamb of God!" This roused him, and with the energy of a dying believer, he terminated the sentence, "... which taketh away the sin of the world." These were his last words.

ROBERT GLOVER (A Martyr) - A.D. 1557
When within sight of the stake, he was suddenly so filled with a sense of God's love and presence, that he clapped his hands, crying out to his friend, "Austin, He is come; He is come!"

CARDINAL MAZARIN - A.D. 1661

"Oh, my poor soul! What will become of thee? Whither wilt thou go? Were I to live again, I would be a capuchin [missionary] rather than a courtier."

REV. J. FLETCHER - A.D. 1785

"Oh, dear Polly, 'God is love!' Shout, shout aloud! Oh, the thought so fills me! I want a gust of praise to go to the ends of the earth." One said, "Do you think that the Lord will raise you up again?" He strove to answer, "Raise in resur... raise in resur...."

REV. E. Y. HUMELBAUGH - A.D. 1868

"Oh, king of terrors! End of time! Oh, all is bright! I'll soon be at home." In a few moments his pulse was still forever.

H. W. FOX - A.D. 1848

"Lord, when Thou wilt, where Thou wilt, as Thou wilt!"

T. H. STOCTON

"I shall receive the crown of glory."

REV. W. EVANS

"I am weakness itself, but I am on the Rock. I do not experience those transports that some have expressed in the view of death, but my dependance is on the mercy of God in Christ. Here my religion began, and here it must end."

WILLIAM HUNTER (A Martyr) - A.D. 1555

Said the sheriff, "If thou wilt recant, thou shalt live; if not, thou shalt be burned!" With steadfast faith and determination he replied, "I will not recant, God willing." He then prayed, "Son of God, shine upon me." His last words were, "Lord, Lord, receive my spirit!"

LATIMER - A.D. 1555

"Be of good comfort, Master Ridley, and play the man! We shall this day light such a candle, by God's grace, in England, as, I trust, shall never be put out!" After this he cried, "Oh, Father of Heaven, receive my soul!"

LEGRAND D'ALLERAY

D'Alleray, an aged representative of France, with his wife, was arraigned before the revolutionary tribunal, during the reign of terror. The judge hinted at an evasive reply to the charge, which the brave old man declined. "I thank you for the efforts you have made to save me; but it would be necessary to purchase our lives by a lie. My wife and myself prefer rather to die. We have grown old together without ever having lied, and we will not do so now, to save a remnant of life."

ARCHBISHOP LEIGHTON - A.D. 1684

"I have a good hope and a great desire to see what they are doing on the other side, for of this world I am extremely weary."

W. STEPHENSON

"Do you see that bright light? Do you see those angels?"

LOUIS XI - A.D. 1783

The king strictly charged his servants, that when they saw him, however ill, they should never dare to name death in his hearing. His physician frequently intimated that death was at hand, upon which the king immediately pressed money into his hand to purchase his silence. The physician is said to have received 55,000 crowns in this way in five months.

DR. VANDERKEMP (An African Missionary)

He closed his eyes, saying with his last breath, "All is well."

EMANUEL SWEDENBORG

"It is well, I thank you. God bless you."

J. L. SCHINDEL

"It is all right, my daughter."

ARCHBISHOP LAUD - A.D. 1645

"I am coming, Lord, as quickly as I can. I know that I must pass through death before I can come to Thee; but it is only the mere shadow of death, a little darkness upon nature!"

LOUISA MAITHER - A.D. 1903

Raising herself up in the bed, she exclaimed, "The Lord wants me to go. I don't know where, but I'm going! Get my slippers, and put them on."

ANDREW FULLER - A.D. 1815

"I have such a hope that with it I can plunge into eternity."

REV. JOHN ANTLE
"The chariot has come, and I am ready to step in."

REV. R. M. McCHEYNE - A.D. 1843
During the delirium immediately preceding his death, he said, "Mind the text, 'Be steadfast, unmoveable, always abounding in the work of the Lord,'" repeating with such emphasis the last clause, "'for as much as ye know that your labour is not in vain in the Lord.'" Then he prayed, "This parish, Lord—this people, this whole place—Holy Father, keep through Thine own Name those whom Thou hast given me," and so he died.

SIR JOHN MASON - A.D. 1566
"Were I to live again, I would change the court for a cloister, my privy councillors bustle for a hermit's retirement, and the whole life I have lived in the palace for an hour's enjoyment of God in the chapel."

WASHINGTON - A.D. 1799
"Doctor, I'm dying, and have been dying for a long time; but I'm not afraid to die."

CAPES DE MAUBORG
The democrats offered, with their carbines at his breast, to spare his life if he would serve under the convention. "No," he replied, "I have never fought but for my God and King! Despicable cowards, fire away!"

LULLI - A.D. 1687
He died with a halter around his neck, in sign of repentance. Then he sang the hymn, "Sinner, thou must die!" with tears of remorse and agony.

QUEEN MARY - A.D. 1587
"When I die, Calais will be found written on my heart."

OLYMPIA FULVIA MORATA - A.D. 1555
"I am nothing but joy."

DANIEL MANN
"Now, Lord, one more glance at Thy Word, and then I will tie up the book for my dear mother, and I go to Thee." Mann was a convict hanged for murder, but soundly converted to God in prison. He died in perfect peace.

WILLIAM GIBSON - A.D. 1891
"I cannot pray! Sin, like a mountain, hides the Saviour from me."

MARY NAPPER STEVENSON - A.D. 1905
Her last audible words were, "Blessed Jesus!"

ANTHONY GROVES - A.D. 1853
"I, who am utterly vile, am going to be with Jesus."

MONICA (Mother of St. Augustine)
"Nothing is far from God, and I do not fear that He will not know where to find me at the resurrection." She was alluding to her dying in a foreign land.

JOHN ELLIOTT - A.D. 1687
"Welcome joy! Pray, pray, pray!"

JOHN JANEWAY - A.D. 1657
"If this is dying, dying is sweet."

J. HEWSON
"Come, Jesus, come!"

GEORGE MYERS
"Come, Lord Jesus!"

G. W. VANDWENTER
"I shall soon be gone, but do not weep for me. I am going home to glory."

M. TROTMAN
"These are light afflictions! His grace is sufficient!"

PLINY FISK - A.D. 1825
"Live near to God, dwell in love, and wear out in the service of Christ."

TALLYRAND PERIGORD
"I am suffering the pangs of the damned."

FITCHET - A.D. 1814
"I need no more medicine. I am well."

DAWSON ELLIOTT
One of his last efforts was to repeat the verse of a hymn:

"A beautiful land by faith I see,
A land of rest, from sorrow free;
The home of the ransomed, bright and fair,
And beautiful angels too are there."

A DYING WOMAN
She had frequently heard the words, "How shall we escape if we neglect so great a salvation?" Unfortunately, she put off the thought of death, regarding it as something in the far distance. One Saturday morning her clothing caught fire and was in flames before she was aware of it. A neighbour succeeded in extinguishing the flames, but not until she was very badly burned. Her friends did the best they could for her, but it soon became evident that she was dying. On hearing this, Christian friends hastened to her bedside and began to question her about her soul. She said she was going to hell, and constantly repeated, "Neglectful, oh neglectful!"

These words were repeated hundreds of times, while her face showed that she was suffering more from the thought of meeting God than from bodily pain. She was asked if she could not trust Jesus for her salvation. To this, she shook her head and said, "Neglectful, oh neglectful!" She continued repeating these words until she was unable to speak, and soon afterwards passed into eternity.

LOUISA HARE - A.D. 1910
A young lady who had lived for years in the enjoyment of

holiness of heart, lay dying of lingering disease. One time, after a period of extreme weakness, she opened her eyes, and putting up her hands, clasped the arms of a friend who was bending over her, and with a beaming countenance said, "He doeth all things well, doesn't He?"

BENJAMIN ABBOTT
"Glory to God, I see the heavens open before me."

WILLIE SCOTT - A.D. 1881
Willie was a little boy who had always been inclined to good, although he was never taught to love God. One time a Christian gentleman had dinner with the family, and before the meal asked a blessing on the food, which greatly impressed the child. Afterward he asked his father why he did this, and was told that the gentleman was asking God to bless them in partaking of the food. After this, he would never eat without first saying grace. Shortly after, God called him home, and as he was passing away, he raised his hands and exclaimed, "Oh, Mamma. I'm in my glory!"

MRS. E. DEARN - A.D. 1904
We heard not a murmur escape her lips during her illness. She remarked to some who visited her, "What would I do if I had neglected seeking the Lord until now?" Some of her last words were, "I thank God that I am here in Ireland to help with the work, and tell the story of Jesus and His love to dying humanity. I am gloriously saved and cleansed through the precious blood of Jesus."

MRS. THOMAS EDWARDS - A.D. 1898

Mrs. Edwards was converted in an old-fashioned Methodist camp meeting near Smith's Fall's when she was about 30 years of age. After living a holy life for over 60 years, God called her to her reward. During her sickness, she exhorted all who came in her room to get ready to meet God. As her family gathered around her bed, she bade them all good-bye, and asked them to meet her in heaven. Then raising her hands toward heaven, she shouted, "Glory! Glory! Glory!" and in a few moments was gone.

MARY ANN GILBERT - A.D. 1887

"Jesus has come for me. Jesus has opened a place for me." To a loved one, she said, "I'll be watching for you on the heavenly shore."

JOHN DOWN

"Though I see death approaching, I fear him not."

MRS. WM. McDOWELL - A.D. 1908

The Sunday previous to her death, she testified to being wholly the Lord's. Turning to the congregation, she said, "If I should die before next Sunday, you will know that I have gone to heaven." I don't want anyone to have to wonder where I have gone." On Thursday evening, a prayer meeting was held in her home, in which she joined heartily, while apparently enjoying the best of health. After the meeting, while setting the table, she fell to the floor, and in a moment was in heaven.

MINNIE GARDNER - A.D. 1906

Shortly before she died, she said, "Over me preaching, when I'm cold in death, say nothing good of me, for I'm not worthy. Tell sinners about Jesus, and hasten them to God."

WILLIAM KNIBB - A.D. 1845

"What bliss, to see the clouds dispersed, and the smile of God resting upon me! All is well!"

FLORENCE CROZIER - A.D. 1903

About a week before the angel of death came, it pleased the Lord to give her a vision of heaven. The Saviour appeared to her, and showed her a beautiful robe and a crown of gold, and said, "These are for you." While thus absorbed in the vision, those who stood around her bed heard her say, "Yes, yes. All right! It's worth living for!" Great was the manifestation of divine grace. She suffered without a tear, and calmly talked of death, obtaining from all who were unsaved their promise to meet her in heaven.

Special Contribution By Maurice Rawlings, M.D.

Several years ago, David Mainse gave me a copy of the original 1913-published version of "Pebbles From The Brink" to help with my research. I found it a treasury of testimonies, providing further insights into what lies beyond death's door.

Of course, one of the reasons why deathbed visions are seldom described today is that the family is usually not there to record them. The patient is often placed in intensive care units or areas where the family is not allowed to be in constant attendance, or the patient is on a ventilator and unable to talk. Sometimes a family member will say, "I can't stand to see Mama like this." Instead of deserting, perhaps the family members have to be working; or, in some instances, don't care. (Nor do we hold hands or openly express love as in the old days. Why?)

The main reason, I suppose, is the fact that patients are seldom permitted to die at home these days. As their condition worsens they're sent to hospitals where disinterested medical personnel shy away from anything that smacks of the spiritual. Some disallow dying testimonies as "unscientific," or label them as "terminal delusions," or they may insist that any "experiential apparitions" are the result of hypoxia, acidosis, medication, toxicity, or similar scapegoat.

This defensive mechanism defies the blood analyses for these conditions, sampling done more frequently than ever as the pre-terminal state approaches, and almost never show any consistent or reproducible cause. (Probably because we doctors, regarding death as the ultimate insult to our superior knowledge, refuse to let the dying patient die—Kevorkianism in reverse.)

Even Darwin recanted his theory of evolution on his deathbed, said Lady Hope of Northfield, England. He asked her to speak about "Jesus Christ... and His Salvation."

Samuel Johnston's words were: "Believe a dying man. Nothing but salvation in Christ can comfort you when you come to die." In 1572, the dying statement of John Knox was, "Live in Christ and the flesh need not fear death...."

The literature of previous generations is replete with terminal heavenly experiences. However, negative, hellish ones are also there, often unreported by proud families, afraid that degrading material would be multiplied in the gossip mills. Nor does anyone brag about such things today. It's a slap in the face; an "F" on the report card. Although "wide is the way to destruction," it is probably for the same reason we never hear a hell-funeral preached.

Voltaire cursed his friends to their faces and said, "I must die—abandoned of God and man," as he agonized with illness for two months. Cromwell remarked as he died, "The devil is ready to seduce us; and I am seduced." Charles IX of France, after ordering the massacre of St. Bartholomew, remarked on his deathbed, "I know not what I am. What shall I do? I am lost." As he died, Napoleon Bonaparte confessed, "What an abyss between my deep misery and the eternal Kingdom of Christ."

And so it goes through history. To mention more recent events, one patient (T.F.), offering his physician all of his possessions for a recovery, was surprised horribly with an unfriendly apparition. "My God," he said, as he continued to stare in dreadful astonishment, mouth open, eyes protruding, until he died. Patient J.B. said, "Devils are in my room." When offered help, he replied, "It is no use. It is too late." Mr. Bartholomy, recovering consciousness for the first time in a week of coma, said in terror, "They're coming again... they're prowling around over there... waiting for me to die."

Of course, the positive, glorious deathbed experiences are like the sands of the sea. The experiencing patients are overjoyed, even exhilarated, at what they see and hear and want others to know, to share their experience. The reports are innumerable and start with various introductions: "I see them, do you? It's wonderful!" Or, "The light is brilliant; the shadows are gone." Some say, "See Him on the Cross?" Or, in some of the old ones, "The chariots have come." Many older ones are recorded in "Pebbles From The Brink" and some of the recent ones in my book, "To Hell and Back." Thank God for these cases and for the revelation of where our loved ones go. Here's a story of a patient of mine which I've included in my book:

While on my hospital rounds one morning, I entered the room of Mrs. Williams. Her minister was with her, quietly reading from the Bible. With her eyes held tightly closed, she asked the minister to stop reading and turn down the bright lights. "But the lights are not on," the minister said. "Then the sun is too bright. Turn down the blinds." She finally opened her eyes and pointed: "I see Him! He's here! See His hands! See the heavenly hosts! They're all here—Majesty unutterable! The most glorious morning of my life," she said, welcoming them. Slowly she eased back, the heartbeat fading, and the breathing stopped. Everything stopped, but the smile persisted.

In the medical profession, we don't encounter atheists in the emergency room and seldom on the deathbed, much less in foxholes. It's always, "God help me" when we are in trouble. Trouble is a time when we want release from pain or misery, but oncoming death is something more: It is a time when people become consumed with thoughts of their eternal destiny. Those who are fearful of what lies beyond are very open to some "Good News."

Dr. Maurice Rawlings is a specialist in cardiovascular diseases at the Diagnostic Center and the area hospitals of Chattanooga, Tennessee. He also teaches for the American Heart Association at university hospitals in the U.S. and Canada. His extensive research in near-death experiences has resulted in his authoring four books: "Beyond Death's Door"; "Before Death Comes"; "Life Wish"; and "To Hell and Back" (Thomas Nelson Publishers).

A Message From David Mainse

My life is forever impacted by the last words of one dying person in particular...my mother. It was late Sunday afternoon, January 17, 1948. The call came for Dad to come to the hospital as quickly as possible and to bring the children. Father drove our new Chevrolet as fast as he dared over the treacherous, icy roads. Mother was still alive when we got to her room, and it was obvious that the nurses had been doing their best to keep her there until we arrived. As soon as we stepped into the room, they took their instruments and departed.

When we were gathered around her bed, all of us in tears, mother looked from one to another, and then her gaze rested on me, her twelve-year-old son. With her remaining strength she spoke her last word, "David." Then I said something that surprised me: "I'll meet you in heaven, Mother. I will! I will!" She smiled and sighed and was gone. Heaven then became a reality for me, because she was there. I was determined to see her again some day. Are you ready to cross the river of death — into eternity? If you are not sure, you can be. Please follow carefully the Bible verses and the prayer that follows:

The Bible says, *"For God so loved the world that He gave His only begotten Son, that whosoever believes in Him should not perish, but have everlasting life"* (John 3:16).

You can receive salvation by believing in Jesus. This is the kind of believing a bride does when she says, "I will" and "I do," and she gives her life to her bridegroom. Just think about it. This salvation includes turning from sin and a self-centred life (repentance) and giving the direction of your life over to Jesus.

Will you decide now? Don't delay. Your crossing of the river could happen anytime. Please be ready.

Here are three steps. Jesus, John and Paul will help you take these steps:

1. Our Lord Jesus said, *"But as many as received Him, to them He gave the right to become children of God, even to those who believe in His name"* (John 1:12).

2. The Apostle John wrote, *"If we confess our sins, He is faithful and just to forgive us our sins and to cleanse us from all unrighteousness"* (1 John 1:9).

3. The Apostle Paul wrote, *"For whoever calls upon the name of the Lord will be saved"* (Romans 10:13).

If you have not yet invited Jesus to be your Saviour, that is your number one need. Salvation cannot be earned; it is a gift from God! Therefore, you need to receive God's gift. Begin by thanking Him now for His gift of eternal life. Then ask Him to forgive your sins. He knows your heart and will answer your prayer.

Will you pray these words with me? Read them as a prayer, out loud if possible:

"Lord Jesus, I confess that I am a sinner, and I ask for Your forgiveness. Thank You for dying on the cross for my sins. I open my life and receive You now as my Saviour and Lord. Thank You for forgiving my sins and giving me eternal life. Take control of my life. Make me the kind of person You want me to be. Amen."

Welcome to His family! Believe that God has heard your prayer. Now, based on His promises you can say the following: 1) I believe that I am His child; 2) I believe that He has forgiven me and made me clean in His sight; and 3) I believe that I am saved!

Here's one more very important Bible quote: *"...if you confess with your mouth the Lord Jesus and believe in your heart that God has raised Him from the dead, you will be saved. For with the heart one believes to righteousness, and with the mouth confession is made to salvation"* (Romans 10:9,10).

Therefore, you need to tell someone right away what you've just prayed and confessed. May I offer you our 24-hour telephone prayer lines?

Please call Crossroads/ "100 Huntley Street" and inform one of our prayer partners of your decision. We will be pleased to provide you with some helpful information (Bible studies, if you request them) to establish you in your new relationship with Jesus and help you grow in your faith. We can also recommend a good church in your area for fellowship, Bible study and spiritual growth. Call our 24-hour prayer line nearest you.

CROSSROADS PRAYER LINES

British Columbia

(604) 430-1212

Prairies

(403) 284-4721
(403) 944-0742

Ontario & U.S.A.

(905) 335-0100
(416) 929-1500

Quebec

(514) 935-8814
(418) 864-7448

Atlantic Canada

(902) 455-2600

— Notes —